"Scholarly and very persuasive"

"Katherine Haubert's work on women in the Bible and the implications for leadership is scholarly and very persuasive. It is also designed to assist Christians to work through the biblical material and its implications. I have found it a most useful resource and commend it highly."

Vinay K. Samuel
Church of South India, Executive Director of the
International Fellowship of Evangelical Mission
Theologians, Oxford, U.K.

"Useful, careful and thoroughly biblical"

"Many thoughtful Christians throughout the world have already benefited from a careful study of this helpful book. It is a useful, careful and thoroughly biblical review of one of the most critical issues of our time—the appropriate roles and ministries of women. I recommend it."

Roberta Hestenes
President and Professor of Christian Spirituality,
Eastern College, St. Davids, Penn.

"Should be heard by all"

"Katherine Haubert has accepted the hard challenge of scrutinizing the most contentious texts of Scripture in the debate about the role of women in the leadership of the church. Her treatment is vigorous and committed, while careful and scholarly. She understands that true biblical interpretation always confronts the reader with his or her own prejudices, and that it is essential to understand oneself anew. Her work is a critical argument for the reality of women's leadership in the church, and should be heard by all who wish to be open to God's word on the subject."

Gordon McConville
Lecturer and author, Oxford University, U.K.

"Allows us to hear the Word of God afresh"

"What does the Bible really teach about women in leadership? Most Christians have inherited assumptions concerning what the Bible has to say on the subject, but very few have taken time to look at the texts carefully with an open mind. Katherine Haubert provides us with an opportunity to examine the basic texts in a manner that allows us to hear the Word of God afresh and also to draw connections to the contemporary reality of shared leadership by women and men in the work of the Kingdom.

"What we have is not a dogmatic exposition of a theological perspective on the subject, but rather an exegetical tool or a study guide to enable us to arrive at our own conclusions on the basis of firsthand observation of the very words of Scripture rather than inherited traditions about the teaching of Scripture. I warmly commend this handbook to all who are interested in the subject."

W. Ward Gasque
Provost and Professor of Biblical Studies, Eastern College, St. Davids, Penn.

Women as Leaders

Accepting the challenge of Scripture

Katherine M. Haubert

MARC

121 East Huntington Drive, Monrovia, California 91016-3400 USA

WOMEN AS LEADERS
Accepting the challenge of Scripture

Katherine M. Haubert

Published by MARC, a division of World Vision International, 121 East Huntington Drive, Monrovia, California 91016 USA

Printed in the United States of America. Cover design by Carol Stickley, Claremont, California.

ISBN 0-912552-81-6

CONTENTS

INTRODUCTION

Women as leaders in the church is not merely an issue of rights and privileges, nor do I address it solely with a desire to see a segment of society liberated or to effect social and moral change.

While these elements are important, I have a broader objective in view. Because they are integral members of the body of Christ, women and their ministries are linked to the fulfillment of God's desire to reveal his glory. This topic, therefore, has implications affecting the hastening of the day in which the "earth will be filled with the knowledge of the glory of the Lord, as the waters cover the sea" (Hab. 2:14).

Ephesians 3:21 tells us that God's glory, his revealed and manifest presence, is made known in the church, the many-membered body of Christ. God's purpose is that through this glorious church, "the manifold wisdom of God should be made known" (Eph. 3:10).

How will this occur?

Hebrews 1:3 describes Jesus as "the radiance of God's glory and the exact representation of his being . . ." It is this Christ, alive within individuals and within the corporate church, who is the hope of realizing that glory (Col. 1:27). As each member of the body of Christ allows the expression of Christ to come forth, the divine presence will be revealed.

This expression is a process that is nothing less than our growth "until we all reach unity in the faith and in the knowledge of the Son of God and become mature, attaining to the whole measure of the fullness of Christ" (Eph. 4:13).

In the church today, the idea of women as leaders faces multifaceted challenges. The ability of women to meet these challenges successfully has a direct bearing on the local church. If the church does not allow women to function freely or to exercise their distinctive giftings and endowments of the Holy Spirit, they will not mature. The result will be an improperly adapted and harmonized church.

Stunted growth and faulty adaptation hamper the richest measure of the divine presence in the church and leave the structure of God's holy temple incomplete (Eph. 2:21-22). Because many women (and men), as "living stones," are not properly fitted into the structure of the spiritual house (1 Pet. 2:5), God's wonderful deeds, virtues, and perfections are not adequately set forth and displayed in the world.

Overcoming obstacles

The purpose of this small book is to enable the saints to overcome any obstacles regarding women as leaders that may hinder the full potential of God within his body. My desire is to take steps toward realizing a church that is ". . . filled to the measure of all the fullness of God" (Eph. 3:19) that all might live to the praise of his glory (Eph. 1:12, 14) who is the "Father of glory" (Eph. 1:17).

I present this book with the realization that many inquiries about women as leaders have not received adequate responses.

The questions presented in the major headings of this work represent most of the concerns of a cross-section of people surveyed in 1988. While this book does not deal with all the issues raised by that survey, there should be adequate material to provide direction for further study.

Each chapter follows the same pattern

Each chapter heading poses a question and refers to related Scriptures. It may be helpful to read the Scripture verses before going on to consider the answers.

The opening paragraphs of the chapter present the challenge. The purpose of the challenge is to inform the reader of problems resulting from an inadequate answer to the chapter question. I intend to challenge the reader to an alternate understanding of the issue.

After this I present various aspects of the issue. This is the main body of the chapter, aimed at providing a brief answer to the question; it is by no means final or complete.

Suggested questions for personal reflection or group discussion are provided (in italics).

At the end of each chapter I provide the response as an opportunity for interaction and application.

Two worksheets are included in the paper: one after chapter five and the other after chapter ten. I offer these as a review.

ONE

IS GOD MALE OR FEMALE?

John 4:1-26; Mark 12:18-25

While this appears to be an unusual question, it is pertinent to the issue of women as leaders. In some circles, there is a tendency to think of God as a male deity. This tendency does have some credibility based on the frequent use of masculine language when referring to God.

Furthermore, Jesus became incarnate as a man, and all the apostles he chose were men as well. Understandably then, some people assume that God is more like man than he is like woman and that man is created in the divine image to a greater degree than woman.

The problem this presents for women as leaders, particularly in the church, is the assumption that naturally follows this train of thought: Since a minister, or a leader in the church, stands in God's place, then that individual must be a man. Why? Because, according to this perspective, "to stand in God's place is to stand in a masculine place."[1]

The implications for women are obvious

When we perceive God in this way there are several repercussions. The implications for women as leaders are obvious. Female leadership would not be an option within a church embracing this viewpoint. In addition, women would tend to feel alienated and estranged from God. They would be viewed as only distantly associated with God and looked down upon as inferior, as is true in later Judaism.[2]

And, of course, the implications regarding biblical interpretation would be disturbing. To classify God according to gender based on imagery and analogy would be a shortsighted limitation of God's nature. Interpretation without recognition of these literary forms could result in unintended conclusions.

Consider Psalm 103:13. What does this image of God communicate to you? How does it help you understand God? What might be some limitations of this image?

In no other area of literature is imagery as important as it is in biblical literature.[3] Since the Bible is God's authentic message to humanity, careful interpretation and understanding of its language is a matter of extreme importance.

To begin down this pathway of understanding, one must realize that the Bible is an Oriental book, and, generally speaking, Oriental literature abounds in imagery. It is resplendent with the simile, metaphor, allegory, and many other figures of speech. Oriental literature delights in such literary practices.[4]

Biblical literature overflows with imagery

One would expect then that the Bible would be filled with this type of speech since it deals with important, lofty truths.[5] The biblical intent is to express these truths and to communicate something of the nature of God. How does God convey himself and express truth in understandable terms to finite beings? The best way is through pictorial forms that help a person relate the unknown to something concrete within his or her experience.[6] Thus biblical literature overflows with this type of language.

Besides the Oriental tendency toward imagery, one must admit that there is really no other form of language with which to speak of God.[7] How can a person understand God unless divine characteristics and attributes are related to the realm of one's understanding? Making this connection is the specific task of biblical imagery.

All this should be kept in mind when pointing out that the Bible refers to God with masculine pronouns and with masculine and feminine terms. Yahweh is called a "husband" (Isa. 54:5) and a "father" (Mal. 1:6), and likened to a "mother" (Isa. 49:14,15).

These are metaphorical descriptions portraying God with human characteristics and motivations. As is typical of this type of language, the metaphor cannot be applied too literally. How then does one decide its intention? The intent of the message is an indicator.

For example, the purpose of Isaiah 54:5 is not to ascribe sexuality to God, but to show his jealous and enduring love. This conclusion is consistent with the message of the chapter as well as the book of Isaiah. Likewise, God is likened to a father in Malachi merely to communicate the right to receive respect from his people.[8] Similarly, God is compared to a nursing mother to show his compassion and inability to forget his own, and not in any effort to feminize him.

Metaphors do not apply in all points

Figurative comparisons are not parallel in all points. Drawing the parallel beyond its intention damages the figure or analogy and does injustice to Scripture. For example, if we take "All flesh is grass" (Isaiah 40:6, NASB) literally, it would be an absurd statement. Isaiah did not use this metaphor to teach that flesh and grass are equal. Rather, he taught that flesh was similar to grass in one way and in one way only: both of them fade away and are temporary.

The metaphor helps the reader understand this point. The author did not intend other similarities to be drawn from this parallel any more than masculine or feminine descriptions were intended to ascribe a specific gender to God. It is just as foolish to take Isaiah's statement literally in all aspects as it is to take descriptions of God literally in all their aspects. Male terminology and male and female imagery merely express aspects of God's character that would otherwise be far beyond the grasp of human understanding.

Why then does the Bible consistently refer to God as "he"? The personal pronouns "he," "him," and "his" have had a general meaning in the English language until recently, in much the same way as "man" has been used in a general way to mean "humanity." Paul Jewett points out that this may be the meaning in Scripture as well.[9]

God is not an "it"

The purpose is to emphasize the personal character of God. The point, as Jewett says, is that "God is not an 'it.' God is a personal being and a personal pronoun must be used to convey that aspect of his nature. . . .

Thus it remains proper to speak of God as 'he.' But it is *necessary* that we strive for precise understanding of what such usage implies and what it does not imply about the nature of God."[10]

Scripture speaks of God as *man* so that people would not understand him as a thing or as an impersonal creature but as one who is in personal relationship with his people. This way of speaking is merely a concession to our lack of understanding. God clearly stated, "I am God, and not man" (Hos. 11:9). "God is not man. God is simply God. He has no sexual characteristic; and that distinguishes him immediately from all the other gods of the ancient world."[11] However, he does embody characteristics that Scripture sometimes identifies as masculine and at other times as feminine.

> List masculine and feminine terms and images used for God. What attributes and characteristics may God be trying to convey by using these figures of speech?

Admittedly, the Bible speaks of God in masculine terms and with female imagery. But in all this God is merely being described in a way that people can understand. At times we see him as a strong, protective patriarch (2 Sam. 7:14), a warrior (Isa. 42:13), and as a king (Isa. 6:1). Then the Bible portrays him as a triumphant leader of an army (1 Sam. 17:45), riding a cherub and scattering the enemy (Ps. 18:10, 14). He stands strong and tall, willing and able, the epitome of masculinity.

God is also portrayed in clearly feminine terms

On the other hand, Scripture portrays God in clearly feminine terms as the one who gave birth to humanity (Deut. 32:18) and cried out in birth pains (Isa. 42:14). Israel was carried in the womb of God (Isa. 46:3-4) and God provided Israel with maternal comfort (Isa. 66:12-13).[12]

While there is an abundance of this type of language in Scripture, the Old Testament is careful to distinguish these descriptions of God from pagan images. In pagan religions, many figurines emphasized the genitalia of the deities, showing that these religions held a biological view of creation. In contrast, the Old Testament portrays Yahweh as non-sexual. It is precisely at this point that Scripture is in contention with paganism.

In this regard, many images in the Bible contradict those of ancient Near East gods. For example, creation was the result of God's word, not a biological function. The male and female references in the Old Testament are figures of speech and are not intended to portray sexuality in God.[13]

Consider the fact that Jesus came as a male. Why? What effect does this have on our understanding of God?

It was important for Jesus to enter the earthly scene as a male to fulfill his divine mission and destiny. There are at least two reasons for this.

First, to fulfill the promises and typology of the Old Testament, Jesus had to be male.

Second, women were rarely allowed to be seen publicly, much less to teach, to speak in a synagogue, or to lead. The tremendous restraints placed on women would not have allowed interaction in the social structure of Jesus' day.

Focus on maleness would have hindered redemption

Furthermore, when looking at texts referring to Jesus as Son of Man, the emphasis falls upon his humanity.[14] Why? Because undue focus on his maleness would have hindered women from fully participating in the redemptive ideal that Christ offered. Jesus ultimately came as the "last Adam" representing humankind (1 Cor. 15:45). As such, he represents male and female as well as Jew and Gentile.

That Jesus came as a male is not to be interpreted as a negative commentary on women any more than that he was a Jew implies that Gentile men are any less like God. Because Jesus came as a Jew does not mean that God is Jewish. Because Jesus came as a man does not mean that God is male. God merely entered the stream of human life in a way that was acceptable to the historical and cultural setting in which the Incarnation took place.

The biblical language appears to affirm this conclusion. The Bible always refers to Jesus' earthly nature as *anthropos* (human; man as a species) but never as *aner* (which can be translated as male).[15] This suggests that New Testament writers consistently used *anthropos* to refer to Jesus because it is his full humanity that is the biblical concern, not his maleness.

Consider your perception of God. When you hear the word "God," what visual images come to mind? What do these images tell you about your relationship to God? Do you think you have a fairly balanced view of who God is? Consider Scripture verses in this section that might help balance your understanding. Meditate on these and ask for the Holy Spirit's guidance (Eph. 1:17-18).

TWO

ARE WOMEN INFERIOR?

Genesis 1 & 2

The challenge for the church today is to throw off the spiritual, emotional, and psychological restraints that have been used to imprison women behind the bars of inferiority.

Many segments of the church have not allowed women to function in leadership roles based on their supposed subordinate position and inherent inferiority. This negative concept of women often finds its justification in the creation accounts of Genesis. A supposed *order of creation* and an assumed purpose in creation lay the groundwork. It claims that because the male was created first, he has an essential priority. Woman is secondary to man because she was formed last.

Consequences of a misinterpreted creation story

This concept goes further by theorizing that the purpose in creating woman was to fulfill a servile role to man. The net result of these beliefs is a hierarchical scale of dominion and submission that makes it unnatural for a man to submit to or obey a woman but not vice versa.[16]

Thus male superiority is given an acceptable social garb; the church approves the lack of mutual submission; female inferiority is imbedded into the fiber of womanhood; gifts of the Holy Spirit lie dormant; and many churches suffer unnecessary constraints.

What is a hierarchy? Can you think of any structures that might be hierarchical? What does this have to do with inferiority?

To understand woman's status, it is important to look at the hierarchical worldview that fosters an inferior perception of women. According to this worldview that has dominated history, life is understood in terms of an ascending and descending order. The higher up a person is on the hierarchical scale or ladder, the greater his or her value and importance. This model is based on order, "a pecking order in which the direction of flow is from superior to subordinate, and not the other way around."[17] On this ladder, traditional theology has placed woman below man: first God, then man, then woman, followed by children, and so on.

According to Webster's dictionary, "inferior" means "situated lower down or nearer" to "what is regarded as the bottom or base . . . of lower degree or rank . . . of less importance, value or merit: of poorer quality."[18]

A hierarchy might imply that women are inferior

This is exactly what the hierarchical scale does: it places people in ascending or descending order on an imaginary ladder of priority and importance. Women are "situated lower down or nearer . . . the bottom" of the ladder than men.[19] Thus although most churchgoers would not express it verbally, this worldview clearly implies that women are inferior. Women are nearer the bottom or base. Many in the church today theologically embrace this view.[20]

What might be an alternate biblical view?

This model represents a presumed, *a priori* stance that is not necessarily a scriptural one. A relational world view is an alternative that is more consistent with God's message. From this viewpoint the important element in God's plan is not an overriding order. Caring, loving, personal relationships replace superiority and inferiority. Relationships, not priority and order, form the structure of God's economy. Paul K. Jewett captures the essence of this perspective:

> Men and women are *persons* related as partners in life. Hence neither men nor women by nature are born to command or obey; both are born to command in some circumstances, to obey in others. And the more personal the relationship between them, the less there is of either; the less personal the relationship between them, the more there is of both.[21]

The creation accounts in Genesis bear this out. Instead of teaching the subordination of woman to man, Genesis 1 and 2 tell of the beauty and the uniqueness of mutual interpersonal relations. There is no evidence of positioning individuals on a hierarchical scale at any level.

Consider the two creation accounts (Gen. 1:26-28 and Gen. 2:18-25). What does the Bible say about the relationship between male and female? Their value before God? Their equality?

Genesis 1 and 2 teach a relational dynamic as the foundation for understanding the roles of man and woman. Equally created in God's image, man and woman reflect this image in their interrelatedness (1:26-27; 2:22-24).[22] God said, "Let us make man [singular] in our image . . . male and female he created them [plural]" (1:26-27).

The emphasis is not only on their diversity, but more importantly on the unity of Adam and Eve. As complements to one another, and in relationship to each other, both are needed to reflect God's image.[23] This unity is further emphasized when we understand "man" as "humankind," an appropriate translation in this text.[24] When he saw the quality of this pair, "God blessed them" (1:28).

The idea of blessing relates to "bowing the knee"

The Old Testament concept of blessing involves attaching high value to the one being blessed, picturing a special future for them and being actively committed to the fulfillment of that blessing.[25] In blessing Adam and Eve, God attached high value to them. He was attributing honor to them. The idea of blessing is related to "bowing the knee," an action showing esteem to an important person.

Not only were Adam and Eve equally created in God's image, they were also equally enfolded in the divine blessing. Both were important. Both were esteemed to be of high value. Both were crowned with divine honor. Both were objects of heavenly concern and participants in a special future. To both of them, God actively committed himself to seeing their special future realized. This was a future in which the blessed will have equal part in multiplying the blessing and filling the earth with the glory of God.[26]

Genesis 2 reinforces the value and interrelatedness of man and woman. In 2:18, God said, "I will make a helper suitable for him [Adam]."

In referring to woman as a suitable helper, God is not positioning woman below man, nor is he implying that woman is secondary. "Help" ("helper," NIV) means "to help, aid, assist; as one succors the miserable and destitute."[27] The Old Testament uses this word most frequently when describing God bringing relief and aid to his people.[28]

Woman is a "suitable help"

This term is significant because it does not carry with it the idea of submission.[29] Being a "suitable help" shows that woman is a help who is equal to, or corresponding to, man.[30] There is no hint of a hierarchical relationship here, nor in the rest of the chapter.

Some commentators consider the naming of the woman by man as proof of man's authority over woman (Gen. 2:23). The power of naming, they claim, implies authority. This interpretation seems based on the social realities of the ancient Near East. Yet it loses credibility because of its failure to consider the thrust of the Hebrew narrative.

The narrative is concerned with bringing the creation of humankind to its culmination, which does not take place until the creation of woman (vv. 22-24). In the Hebrew text, God's statement, "It is not good for man to be alone. I will make a helper suitable for him" (v. 18), creates a tension. Then the animals were brought to Adam and named (vv. 19, 20). In naming the animals, he was not exercising authority over them but identifying the relationship and significance they had to him.

Immediately following the naming, verse 20 concludes, "But for Adam no suitable helper was found." The animals did not stand in relationship to man as a suitable helper. They did not meet man's need for a complement. The inclusion of the naming process emphasizes this fact, and highlights the incompletion of creation at this point. Thus the tension remains. To introduce the notion of authority here is foreign to the text.[31]

"She shall be called woman"

When Adam cried out, "She shall be called 'woman,'" he was identifying the relationship and significance she had to him. Sarna brings out this thought:

> Here the man gives her a generic, not a personal, name, and that designation is understood to be derived from his own, which means he acknowledges woman to be his equal. Moreover, in naming her *'ishah'*, he simultaneously names himself. Hitherto he is consistently called *'adam'*, he now calls himself *'ish'* for the first time. Thus he discovers his own manhood and fulfillment only when he faces the woman, the human being who is to be his partner in life.[32]

Now the tension is resolved. There is a release as man declares, "This is now bone of my bones and flesh of my flesh" (v. 23). Among the living creatures, man has recognized the one who is like him.

Because man was created first, according to the account in Genesis 2, some have assumed that he is superior to woman. If we follow this reasoning, then because of Genesis 1 we would have to conclude that the heavens and earth, the plants, fish, birds, and land animals have priority over humanity. After all, humanity was created last, *subsequent* to these other things.

Precedence in creation does not indicate superiority

But the fact remains that the reverse is true. Humanity is the high point of God's handiwork, not the low point. Thus woman's creation after man (Gen. 2), if it indicates anything at all, would indicate that she is superior to him! However, the intention of the text is not to prove the superiority of one over the other, but to portray the complementary relationship between man and woman. There is something in this beautiful blend of harmonious relationship that reflects God.[33]

The fact that woman comes from man (2:21) only proves her likeness to him. She is of the same substance. In 2:23, Adam declares his likeness to Eve and highlights their mutuality. In delight he cries out, "This is now bone of my bones, and flesh of my flesh," a statement known as a "formula of relationship."[34]

He then refers to Eve as "woman," one like himself. Finally, their joining as "one flesh" (v. 24) emphasizes their oneness and equality. It is upon this unity and mutuality that God pronounces his blessing (see Psalm 133).

> *It may help the reader to imagine himself or herself in God's "shoes." You have finished your creation task. You have just created man and woman, and you want to write a report on the results of the job. How do you feel about your creation (good-bad, satisfactory-unsatisfactory)? How do you feel toward your creation, man and woman (love-hate, indifference-caring)? What would you do to preserve your creation?*
>
> *Make a personal application of your response. What value do you think God places on you? On others around you? On women in general? How should this affect your relationships?*

THREE

WHAT ABOUT THE FALL?

Genesis 3

For thousands of years theologians have interpreted the Fall as the basis for a demeaning theology of womanhood.[35] The reasoning is the perception that Eve was the cause and source of Adam's deception.

Woman was seen as intrinsically evil, gullible, deceived and deceiving, unfit for intellectual pursuit or leadership roles. Tertullian called woman the "Devil's gateway," the one who destroyed "God's image, man."[36] This attitude in the church has encouraged a negative view of woman, placed the responsibility for sin and deception on her shoulders, and given her a subordinate role.

The church often justifies the subjugation of woman because of God's pronouncement in Genesis 3:16, "Your desire will be for your husband, and he will rule over you." Under this guise some consider it appropriate for a man to lord it over a woman. Not only does the church accept domination on this basis, it also frequently rejects female leadership for the same reason. The abuse of power and control becomes an issue.

Why was Eve chosen as Satan's target for temptation? Does this mean she was responsible for the first sin?

Genesis 3 gives a clear picture of how the Creator's intent was deferred, the blessing hindered, and relationships marred. In 3:1-4, the serpent approached Eve and began a conversation with her. There is no evidence that Eve was Satan's target because of her gullibility, inability, or proneness to deception. There is no biblical statement to this effect.

The previous chapter had just emphasized woman's strength and capability. "Suitable helper" (Gen. 2:18) is a phrase used to describe a "stronger party who comes in to support a weaker party."[37] Being suitable, woman is sufficient and adequate, as is man, for fulfilling God's design of fruitfulness and dominion (Gen. 1:28, KJV). The man's "cleaving" in Genesis 2:24 (KJV) is used almost invariably to describe a "weaker cleaving to a stronger. It is used of Israel, cleaving to God (e.g., Josh. 23:8; Ps. 91:14), but never the other way around."[38]

Woman is not depicted as weak, unstable

These descriptions, while not intending to display the dominance of either gender, places woman in a very positive position alongside man. We do not see woman as a weak, unstable creature.

It is also an unfair treatment of the text to say that woman is the temptress of man. Woman handed the fruit to man apparently without a word (3:6). Without a word man consented to eat it. There is no record of a conversation, nor is there evidence of an attempt to persuade or cajole man into disobedience. Seemingly without a word, without resistance or hesitation, man accepted the fruit and ate it. Why such willingness to consort in this misdeed? The plural form "you" in the serpent's speech suggests that man was present alongside Eve, and thus he had heard the conversation.[39] Sarna points out that "the Hebrew text here literally means, 'She also gave her husband *with her ('immah)'* suggesting that he was a full participant in the sin."[40]

Genesis 3 continually directs the reader's attention to the human responsibility for wrongdoing. It places this responsibility squarely on the shoulders of man *and* woman: "The eyes of both of them were opened" (3:7). Adam disobeyed God as readily as Eve. It should be noted that it was not until both Adam and Eve ate the fruit that the results of sin came flooding in (v. 7). Neither of them could shift the blame for their wrong, for God held both accountable. Just as they had been equal in creation, so they were equal in their responsibility before God. God called each of them to give an account for their actions (vv. 11-13), and each suffered the consequences of the deeds.

Rule, not by God's design, but by sin's dictate

Genesis 3:16-19 describes these consequences. This description portrays the state of life lived in disobedience to God. It is not a divine command or decree but a statement of how people, tarnished and affected by sin, would live in a fallen world.[41] Because of sin, woman would labor in childbearing and man's work would be toilsome. Woman's desire would be for her husband, that is, either (1) she would long for the perfection of relationship that once was theirs but now seemed far off, or (2) she would desire to usurp his role.[42] And the husband would rule over the wife, not by God's design, but by sin's dictate. The picture is a bleak portrait of the devastating effects of sin on the relationship between man and woman.

Woman in Genesis 3 is not the reason for the Fall. She is not the sly, cunning trickster of man. The willful decision of two free moral agents exercising their liberty independent of each other is the reason for the Fall.[43] Woman is not the gullible culprit any more than man, for sin begins in the hearts of individuals and singularly each person stands before God for his or her deeds (Matt. 12:33-34).

Divine decree did not dictate woman's subjugation to man; forceful control and dominion are evil results of sin. The greater the domination of one person over another, the deeper the evidence of sin, and the greater the perversion of creation's intent.[44]

Is woman inferior because of the Fall?

In Genesis 1 and 2, Adam and Eve lived in an environment of God's blessing, an active force of benefit affirming their equal value and importance. But in Genesis 3 the antithesis to blessing entered the scene. Death and darkness gained entrance through the door of sin. Earth's inhabitants and its environment were dramatically affected. Adam aimed accusation at Eve. Eve cast blame on the serpent. Tension and accusation disrupted the blissful harmony that had embraced this pair. A sense of inferiority had set in (Gen. 3:7).

In an insecure power play, man began to clamor for dominion (3:11-12) and woman would seek to cast off the weight of his restraint. The value, importance and honor that had graced man and woman were marred and obscured. A thorny wreath of shame replaced the crown of honor (3:8).

Was woman now inferior?

No, but the toll of sin immersed her in the depths of an existence that was far from the reflected image of God. The weight of sin began to crush her God-given sense of worth. It subjugated her, and throughout history the damages incurred by sin surfaced over and over again. In the Old Testament she was treated as secondary; she was subordinate and inferior in Judaism; Ancient Greece accepted her as little more than chattel; and by Jesus' time there persisted a low opinion of the value of woman.[45] The influence of sin disrupted the realities of God's blessing.

God's plan had been very different

Was this God's plan? No, God's plan included the fullest measure of his blessing for man and woman. Still, God had a special future envisioned for them. This future would be culminated and secured in Jesus Christ. In blessing, God not only imparted affirmation and envisioned a future, he also actively committed himself to fulfilling that blessing.

Identify one marginalized group in society such as refugees, ethnic minorities, or women. Relate their position to the effects of the Fall. In what ways are they treated differently than others? Does the Fall justify any disparity in treatment?

Internalize your response. Have you ever been unjustly treated or marginalized? How has the sin of others been abrasive to you? Does this mean that you are not blessed and accepted by God? How can you respond in a way that would bring blessing in the midst of perversity?

FOUR

WAS JESUS A WOMEN'S LIBERATIONIST?

Luke 4:18-19; Galatians 3:13-14

Jesus came into the world as the heavenly expression, the "radiance of God's glory" to reveal the will and purpose of his Father (Heb. 1:3). As such he stands as the model of Christendom, the pattern for all people to follow.

Yet ever since the days of his earthly existence, the church has struggled to emulate that divine pattern in relation to its attitude and acceptance of women both in status and in role. Tension has often been drawn between the ideal, Jesus, and the residual effects of the Fall that have shaped cultural thought and structure. Men's dogmas, much like those of the Pharisees, have sought to put a stranglehold on the life and liberty Jesus accorded women.

The challenge for the church is to allow the redeeming results of Calvary and Jesus' attitude to shape its views. The church needs to take the sickle of truth and cut through the "barbed wire of cultural custom and taboo in order to emulate the one who promised both men and women, 'If the Son makes you free, you will be free indeed'!"[46]

In what way or ways was Jesus a liberator of women?

Jesus did not come as a proponent of social justice or as a spokesman for woman's rights *per se*. But he was indeed God's revolutionary agent sent to restore the dignity of all humans.

23

In Luke 4:18-19, Jesus declared his mission: "The Spirit of the Lord is on me, because he has anointed me to preach good news to the poor. He has sent me to proclaim freedom for the prisoners and recovery of sight for the blind, to release the oppressed, to proclaim the year of the Lord's favor."

Sin imprisoned and oppressed humanity. But the Year of Jubilee—the year of the Lord's favor—was when the oppressed were set free. The object of the mission was to sabotage the effects of sin and restore the fullness of God's blessing to men and women (Gal. 3:13-14).

It was on the cross that Jesus bore sin's penalty, for sin had brought dishonor to men and women and had devalued human life. In his act of redemption, Jesus restored honor and esteem to all who would come to him. He was the promised blessing, the blessed one in whom all may be blessed (Gen. 12:2-3; Gal. 3:13-14).

Was Jesus a women's liberationist? Indeed he was THE liberator of humanity and embracer of those in need. He devoted the scope of his life and ministry to restoring individuals, male and female, to full personhood. As such, Jesus was a liberator of woman to a degree far greater than any she had known.

Jesus' treatment of women was revolutionary

In Jesus' day society devalued women. They were of little importance to anyone, secluded and powerless. Social and religious restrictions barred them from the kind of life men knew. Participation in public activity was taboo, discussion with a scholar in the streets a disgrace, teaching and bearing witness forbidden, and being alone with a man out of the question.[47] A married woman could not be looked at or greeted. The religious community of that day clearly marked women as inferior.[48] But Jesus broke through the barriers of religious tradition and social custom.

Against all convention, Jesus reached out to women. He violated the traditional code and the Jewish norm prohibiting men from speaking to women publicly.[49] In John 4:1-42, he accepted a drink from a Samaritan woman, even though Jews believed that Samaritans were unclean. Still, the socially unclean found acceptance in Jesus' presence. A woman with an issue of blood touched him. He welcomed her, contrary to ancient laws dictating her touch to be unclean (Matt. 9:20-26; Mark 5:24-34; Luke 8:40-56).

Jesus also touched women publicly, an uncustomary act in Jewish society (Luke 13:10-17), and openly taught them when most rabbis shunned it as unacceptable (Luke 10:38-42). Jesus found that women could understand God's truth. The Lord commended Mary for her desire to learn (Luke 10:38-42). While "Martha was doing a really feminine job, . . . Mary was behaving just like any other disciple."[50] On the other hand, Martha's confession of Jesus as the Son of God is commendable and closely paralleled Peter's confession (cf., John 11:27 and Matt. 16:16).

Women were warmly accepted as disciples

Women were warmly accepted into the ranks of discipleship, often travelling with Jesus and supporting him financially (Mark 15:40-41; Luke 8:1-3). His teaching included objects and illustrations familiar to them, such as wedding feasts, childbirth, yeast, sewing, and grinding corn. He even used feminine imagery to describe God (Luke 15:8-10).[51]

The stories he used had appeal to men and women, inviting everyone to receive and respond to his message. He often emphasized a point by telling two similar stories, or using two images, one with a male character and the other with a female one (Luke 11:5-9; 18:1-8; Matt. 24:39-41; Luke 17:34-36; 11:29-32; Matt. 24:45-51; 25:1-13).[52] He clearly meant his teaching for both men and women.

Why were women among Jesus' most devoted followers? Give examples.

In response to Jesus' acceptance, women became some of his most devoted followers.[53] They were the ones who stayed with him during his crucifixion (Mark 15:40-41) and were first to arrive at the empty tomb (Matt. 28:1; Mark 16:1-2; Luke 24:1-12; John 20:1-9). It was Mary who desperately searched for her Lord (John 20:10-16). It was a woman who abandoned all protocol to perform the slave's task of anointing Jesus' feet and wiping them with her hair. It was immodest for a woman to let down her hair, but in the warmth of Jesus' presence she did not care (John 12:1-8).[54]

Mary Magdalene, considered a prostitute by some, acted in a similar way (Luke 7:36-50). Jesus was probably the first man who had treated her with respect and dignity.

The intimacy, warmth, and openness of Jesus' relationship to women seemed always to result in a deep, personal response. Dorothy Sayers, a renowned lay theologian and author, beautifully summed up the significance of this response:

> Perhaps it is no wonder that women were first at the Cradle and last at the Cross. They had never known a man like this Man—there never has been such another. A prophet and teacher who never nagged at them, never flattered or coaxed or patronized; who never made arch jokes about them, never treated them either as "The women, God help us!" or "The ladies, God bless them"; who rebuked without querulousness and praised without condescension; who took their questions and arguments seriously; who never mapped out their sphere for them, never urged them to be feminine or jeered at them for being female; who had no axe to grind and no uneasy male dignity to defend; who took them as he found them and was completely unselfconscious. There is no act, no sermon, no parable in the whole Gospel that borrows its pungency from female perversity; nobody could possibly guess from the words and deeds of Jesus that there was anything "funny" about woman's nature.[55]

Imagine yourself in Jesus' time as one of his disciples. How does his unconditional acceptance cause you to respond to him? How does it make you feel about yourself? Your family? Friends? Should this acceptance affect the way you treat others? Women? Men? Social outcasts? How might these relationships be affected in a positive way?

FIVE

DID PAUL DISLIKE WOMEN?

Galatians 3:26-29; Ephesians 1:3

The church often uses the writings of the apostle Paul to place women in a subordinate status and role. Citing certain passages keeps women out of leadership and under the authority of men in veiled and silent submission. As a result, some would argue, the use of these passages has quenched the smoldering wick of female identity and broken the bruised reed of women's leadership potential, all in the name of biblical authority.

But is this the correct biblical interpretation? This warrants a fresh look at the Scriptures. The challenge for the contemporary church is to reassess the Pauline attitude toward, and doctrine concerning, women in the life of the church.

In his teaching, how did Paul affirm woman's place in the church? (Look at the teaching in one or two of his writings.)

In his teaching, Paul consistently affirmed that women have an essential place in the life of the church. In Romans he taught that by faith in Christ all are united, and he committed the gospel to all races and to both sexes (chapter 16). In Romans and Corinthians both men and women are justified by faith and challenged to live in a new relationship of freedom and dignity, equally gifted and equally able to approach

God. Galatians seeks to abolish divisive distinctions (including that between male and female) and focuses Christian identity in Christ alone.

Women held responsible positions in ministry

In Ephesians, the mutuality of men and women, as modelled by Christ's self-sacrificing love, is the road to unity. Philippians clearly shows that women held responsible positions in ministry, and it appeals for the unanimous adoption of the mind of Christ (not a patriarchical mind-set) that the church's mission might be successful. Colossians calls men and women to mutual responsibility (3:12-13, 18-19). And 1 Timothy offers evidence for the inclusion of women in church office.[56]

According to Paul, women not only *belonged to* the church with equal status and worth as men, they *constituted* the church through the revelation of God in Christ. It is this revelation that radically affects the essential identity and worth of womanhood. Her identity is no longer a reflection of cultural mores, social restrictions, physical form, or hierarchical programming. The face of Christ mirrors her new identity and her worth is matched by the price of his shed blood.

> *In Galatians 3:26-29, what was Paul saying about the relationships between Jew and Greek? Slave and free? Male and female? (Reflect on Ephesians 1:3 in light of this.)*

In Galatians 3:26-29, Paul proclaimed a new identity and an essential unity based on Christian equality. Here he unveiled the divine masterpiece. The brush strokes blend to paint a portrait of the new creature in Christ. This portrait is the divine masterpiece of all who share the Christian faith: Jew and Greek, slave and free, male and female (v. 28). It is the portrait that is to be framed as woman's new identity, for it recaptures the realities of the Creator's original intent (Gen. 1:27-28). The title is "New Creation Realities."

The figure represented is not a restoration of the traditional sexual and cultural patterns. It is a new masterpiece that replaces the scarred faces of racial (Jew-Greek), social (slave-free), and sexual (male-female) antagonism. Because Christ called Christian women, this reality has been purchased for them.

"Sonship" is for all believers

Galatians 3:26 begins with Paul's declaration, "You are all sons of God through faith in Christ Jesus." It is as if Paul were saying, "You are no longer immature children under a custodian ('the law', v. 25), but in Christ you are mature sons with the attending rights and privileges of sonship."[57] Sonship is expressive of the Godward relationship experienced by *all* believers, female and male. Thus Paul identifies the status of believers, a status equally shared by all who are in Christ.

Galatians 3:28 further strengthens the stress upon equality and unity found in verse 26. In this verse Paul makes a revolutionary statement: "There is neither Jew nor Greek, slave nor free, male nor female, for you are all one in Christ Jesus."[58] In Christ, racial, social, and sexual distinctions become irrelevant. Although each individual maintains unique and distinct qualities, all are one.[59] Should these distinctions ferment into discrimination, this oneness will sour. Christian unity can be found in identification with Christ (v. 27), but we break that unity when distinctions dictate the level and extent of one's participation in the life of the church.[60]

Galatians 2:11-21 emphasizes this point. Paul went to great lengths to show that the Gentiles were equal participants in the life of faith, not only spiritually but also socially. Peter had separated himself from the Gentiles according to standard Jewish practice. Paul's stinging accusation flailed Peter, "You are not acting in line with the truth of the gospel" (2:14, author's paraphrase).

What is the truth Paul referred to? The truth is that the doctrinal statement in Galatians 3:26-29 has social application. The old distinctions marking the Jew-Greek relationship no longer dictate how a Jew relates to a Greek in the new community. Being a Jew does not give a person superior status or special rights and privileges that are withheld from others. This is the distinct message of the passage.

Equal standing in Christ is not just for males

In the church, the circumcised are no better off than the uncircumcised. The same holds true for the slave and free, for the male and female. A man does not hold special rights that are withheld from a woman. The social implications of being in Christ are as real for the male and female as they are for the Jew and Greek. Equal standing in Christ is not just a spiritual reality without implications for community living.[61] As the Greeks are granted equal status and participation in the life of the church, so women are granted equal status and participation in the life of the church also. This is the principle established in Galatians 3:28.[62]

In Christ the alienation barring women is removed

In Ephesians 1:3, Paul declared the restoration of blessing in Christ. It is at this juncture of revelation that woman can be lifted from the degradation of sin. She is lifted out of the dregs of worthlessness and inferiority, from beneath the heel of dominion, for the blessing of God graces her again with a crown of honor. Christ removed the alienation that barred her from God. She is connected to the divine blessing that bestows high value on her and pictures a special future for her. She can now know that God is actively at work on her behalf to fulfill the terms of that blessing that envisions a future of fruitfulness and dominion (see Gen. 1:28).

Thus the blessing is woman's promise of a new status and role. It is the promise of a life of full ministry potential (fruitfulness) and a life of authority (dominion) on an equal level with all members of the body of Christ.

Did Paul practice what he preached concerning women? Give examples.

Paul clearly showed that he fully accepted and worked alongside women who engaged in missionary work and exercised leadership in the church. In his letters he addressed house churches associated with women: Apphia in Colossae (Philem. 2), Nympha in Laodicea (Col. 4:15), Priscilla and Aquila in Corinth, Ephesus, and Rome (1 Cor. 16:19; Rom. 16:3) and Chloe in Corinth (1 Cor. 1:11).

In the book of Romans he acknowledged the labors of Mary, Tryphena, Tryphosa, and Persis who occupied a place of prominence in the church (Rom. 16:6, 12).[63] He spoke of Junia as an apostle and highly commended her ministry.[64] He greeted the mother of Rufus, the sister of Nereus, and Julia. Priscilla and her husband worked closely with Paul.[65] Paul called them "fellow workers in Christ," a term emphasizing their joint efforts in proclaiming the good news.[66]

In Philippians he addressed Euodia and Syntyche as "women who have contended at my side in the cause of the gospel" (Phil. 4:2). And he called Phoebe a deacon and leader (Rom. 16:1). According to this evidence, Paul clearly practiced what he preached. (For additional comments on Phoebe, Junia, Euodia, and Syntyche, see chapter ten.)

Picture yourself as a member of the early church. Write an account of a conversation you have just had with a woman outside the Christian community. Tell her about your travels and contact with Paul. What sort of man is he? Describe his attitude toward the women on his ministry teams and his hearty endorsement of women in the life of the church. Be sure to include illustrations of things he has done and said.

REVIEW QUESTIONS

1. Consider Psalm 103:13. What does this image of God communicate to you? How does it help you understand God? What might be some limitations of this image?

2. List masculine and feminine terms and images used for God. What attributes and characteristics may God be trying to convey by using these figures of speech?

3. Consider the fact that Jesus came as a male. Why? What effect does this have on our understanding of God?

4. What is a hierarchy? Can you think of any structures that might be hierarchical? What does this have to do with inferiority?

5. What might be an alternate biblical view?

6. Consider the two creation accounts (Gen. 1:26-28 and Gen. 2:18-25). What does the Bible say about the relationship between male and female? Their value before God? Their equality?

7. Why was Eve chosen as Satan's target for temptation? Does this mean she was responsible for the first sin?

8. What effects did sin have on Adam? on Eve?

9. Is woman inferior because of the Fall? Explain.

10. In what way(s) was Jesus a liberator of women?

11. In what ways was Jesus' treatment of women revolutionary?

12. Why were women among Jesus' most devoted followers? Give examples.

13. In his teaching, how did Paul affirm woman's place in the church? (Look at the teaching in one or two of his writings.)

14. In Galatians 3:26-29, what was Paul saying about the relationships between Jew and Greek? Slave and free? Male and female? (Reflect on Eph. 1:3 in light of this .)

15. Did Paul practice what he preached concerning women? Give examples.

SIX

WHAT DOES HEADSHIP MEAN?

Ephesians 1:22-23; 4:15-16; 5:21-33;
Colossians 1:15-20; 2:19; 1 Corinthians 11:3

Traditionally the church interprets "headship" as "rulership by a person of superior rank or authority." The church accepts this definition as scriptural proof of an *order of creation* in which males are to rule and lead, while females submit and follow.[67]

Such an understanding has tremendous implications for the church and the home. If we embrace this style of headship as the biblical norm, then we naturally bar women from any significant form of leadership. This would dramatically affect the male-female relationship, particularly the one between husband and wife. We would expect women to take a sub-servient role. This attitude fosters an erroneous assumption that there is something inherently inferior about women.

Yet this assumption is not compatible with the concept of equality developed throughout Scripture.[68] The challenge for the church is to confront the inequity it has produced and to reconsider the meaning of headship from a grammatical and contextual basis.

What is the commonly understood meaning of "head?" Do you think this is the biblical meaning? Why?

The Greek word for "head," *kephale*, most often refers to the uppermost part of the human body, but it is also used metaphorically. While in the English language, head figuratively means "chief, boss, or ruler," it shouldn't be assumed that this is the biblical meaning.

Headship means "fountainhead" or "life source"

The Greeks believed that the heart was the ruling organ of the body. They saw it as the seat of the will and emotions, whereas the head served the body by giving it life.[69] Thus a better meaning for head, in a figurative sense, would be "fountainhead" or "life-source."[70]

Gilbert Bilezikian has done an excellent study of this word (*kephale*). He surveys its use in non-biblical writings, in the Greek translations of the Old Testament, and in the New Testament. "Source" or "source of life," he agrees, is the idea it conveys in texts like 1 Corinthians 11:3 and Ephesians 5:23. His conclusion: *kephale* is used metaphorically in the New Testament "in a variety of settings that give it some conceptual flexibility, but always with the notion of serving the body in a creational, nurturing, or representational dimension."[71]

Henry G. Liddell and Robert Scott, in the oldest and most extensive lexicon, list several definitions of *kephale*, none of which expresses authority or superior rank. Rather, the figurative uses (applicable to this study) include words like "source, origin," "crown, completion," and "sum, total." This is how the secular and religous Greeks of Paul's day would have understood the term.[72]

Another commentator, Gordon Fee, sums up the findings of many scholars in his analysis of 1 Corinthians 11:3:

> Indeed, the metaphorical use of *kephale* ("head") to mean "chief" or "person of the highest rank" is rare in Greek literature—so much so that even though the Hebrew word *ro's* often carried this sense, the Greek translators of the LXX [Septuagint] who ordinarily used *kephale* to translate *ro's* when the physical

head was intended, almost never did so when "ruler" was intended, thus indicating that this metaphorical sense is an exceptional usage and not part of the ordinary range of meanings for the Greek word.

Paul's understanding of the metaphor, therefore, and almost certainly the only one the Corinthians would have grasped, is "head" as "source," especially "source of life."[73]

What were some functions of Christ's headship? (Consider Eph. 1:22-23; 4:15-16; 5:21-33; Col. 1:15-20; 2:19.)

Passages where Christ's headship is related to the church portray this meaning.[74] As head of the church in Ephesians 1:22-23, Christ supplies the body with its fullness. The head-body language serves to communicate the church's participation *in* Christ's authority (established in vv. 20-21), instead of Christ's authority *over* the church. While he does have authority over the church, this authority is not the issue in the metaphor. The issue is shared life. Christ fills the body. He is its source of life, the one who brings it to fullness or completion. The body, in turn, is the expression of that fullness.

The head provides for growth, nurture

Ephesians 4:15-16 and Colossians 2:19 communicate a similar idea. In these verses, the function of the head is to provide for the growth, nurture, and upbuilding of the body. It is the life source enabling growth to occur. The body responds by building itself up in love.

The picture in Ephesians 5:21-33 is, again, one of nurture. Christ's headship to the church (v. 23) is paralleled to his love, care, and nurture for the church (vv. 25-33).

Colossians 1:15-20 practically defines the meaning of the word: "He is the head of the body, the church; he is the beginning and the firstborn from among the dead." The idea is that the church finds its beginning in him, the head. It started with him, the firstborn. He is the source—the inception—of its existence.

If these passages show anything at all about Christ's authority, they show that he shares his authority with the church. It is flowing from him and imparted to his people. He is the fountainhead of life, the wellspring from which the body receives all it needs. While there are terms referring to Christ's rulership, as head to the church, Christ is not its ruler but its life source.

The type of headship Christ modeled points toward interrelationship. The idea is that Christ gives himself unstintingly in a creational, nurturing, and supporting way to the church. The church in turn responds with a loving trust and dependence.[75]

> In what sense is man head of woman? A husband head of his wife? Consider Jesus' example of headship.

It is in this context that we should understand male headship. In calling man "head," the Holy Spirit acknowledges, first, that man was the original source of woman's life at creation (just as Christ is described as the "firstborn of all creation," the origin of those in the church). The idea is that man was the Creator's instrument of life to woman (Gen. 2:21). It was from man's rib that she was created.

As applied to the husband-wife relationship, this term implies that the husband provides his wife with nurture, support, bonding, and a loving atmosphere in which to grow. The "husband is the head of the wife as Christ is head of the church" (Eph. 5:23). How does Christ fulfill this role? He is the church's source of life in a creational, nurturing, loving, and supportive way.

Headship is defined in the context of love

The encompassing text bears this out. In the surrounding passage (Eph. 5:21-33), love as illustrated by the self-sacrificing love of Christ defines headship(v. 25). It is the love that motivated Christ to pay the redemptive price (vv. 23, 26-27). It is a love that is nurturing (v. 29) and that produces bonding and unity (v. 31). The husband, as head, pours himself out in "agape" love and in self-sacrificing service for his wife. Also, since the head metaphor includes the body metaphor, the idea is one of reciprocity in which the wife, as the body, reciprocates love in a similar, self-sacrificing lifestyle.

A partnership of giving and receiving

The total picture is one of mutual acceptance and submission, a partnership of giving and receiving.[76] The point is not authority, rulership, or position. The point is the *union* between the head and the body (vv. 28-32). To impose an authoritative structure on this beautiful blend of harmonious interrelationship is to destroy the intention of the metaphor and the meaning of headship itself.[77]

1 Corinthians 11:3 also refers to man as the head of woman. Those who interpret "head" as "boss" inevitably deduce a hierarchical ladder: God ruling over Christ, Christ over man, and man over woman. However, not only does this contradict the fundamental meaning of the term, it also ignores the sentence structure. If a hierarchy was intended, the pairs (Christ-man; man-woman; God-Christ) would have been placed in descending order with the most important pair first and the least important last.[78] 1 Corinthians 11:3 *would have* looked like this: "The head of Christ is God, the head of man is Christ, and the head of woman is man." But this was not done. Instead, it is more likely that a chronological sequence determined the placement of the pairs.[79]

This sequence makes sense when we understand "head" as "source" or "origin." First, in creation, man came from Christ (John 1:3, 10; 1 Cor. 8:6). After the creation of man, woman was formed from him (Gen. 2:22). Then later, on the historical plane, Christ came from God to dwell among men (John 1:14; 8:42). Historically, man came first, then woman, then Christ. The origin of man was Christ; the origin of woman was man; and the origin of Christ was God.[80] While it is uncertain whether this sequence was intentional, the interpretation works well with the structure of 1 Corinthians 11:3.

Not a chain of command

Other portions of the text verify that Paul was not thinking of a chain of command. Verses 8 and 12 explicitly state that woman came *from* man, emphasizing derivation or origin. "This strongly suggests," the Mickelsens conclude, "that Paul was using 'head' in verse 3 with the Greek meaning of source, origin, base, or derivation."[81]

Furthermore, there is a need for consistency in the use of *kephale* in 1 Corinthians 11:3. If we understand this term in one way for the male-female relationship, the same interpretation must be used of the relationship between God and Christ. "It would be acceptable to speak of God as the 'source' or 'origin' of Christ, but not as the 'chief, boss, or ruler'; such a hierarchical order would be more consistent with fourth century Arianism than with the rest of Scripture."[82]

> *What does the concept of Christ as "head" mean to you? How does it affect your relationship to him and your understanding of him? Are there any practical ways you can apply this truth to your life? List them.*

SEVEN

ARE WOMEN SUBORDINATE?

Ephesians 5:21-23; 1 Peter 3:1-7; John 13:1-17

For nineteen centuries in the Christian church women almost invariably had a subordinate position to men.

The most indefensible belief is that all women are subordinate to all men just because they are women. This contradicts the fact that one cannot be subordinate and equal unless that subordination is voluntary, not intrinsic.[83] Also, it can be argued that a one-sided submission of the wife to her husband places an unbiblical imbalance in their relationship. The wife learns how to submit, but not how to mature in other responsibilities such as decision-making. The husband, on the other hand, becomes domineering and fails to learn the true meaning of submission himself.

What does submission mean? List some of its synonyms and antonyms.

When Paul spoke of submission he used a word that describes a "voluntary attitude of giving in, cooperating, assuming responsibility, and carrying a burden."[84] It means to honor and respect another, to prefer another above oneself.[85] In this light, submission looks more like an expression of the God-kind of love, rather than subjection to an authoritarian figure.

Submission is never forced, coerced

While the word submission is used differently in several places, when referring to relationships in the church it always refers to a *willful* deference to others. It is never forced or coerced. It does not involve the idea of unquestioning obedience as much as the thought of putting someone else's concerns, feelings, and thoughts above one's own interests.[86] When submitting, a person considers the advice of others, seeks their input, and yields to their interests.

> *Think about mutual submission. Is it appropriate in the church? The home? How would it affect relationships in these areas?*

There is much stress placed on the submission of women to men and of wives to husbands. Yet Scripture clearly shows that submission must take root on a broader scale. It is not merely the duty of the woman or wife. Mutual submission, adaptation, and coordination are required of *all* people who are in Christ.

The passage in Ephesians on husband-wife relations begins at verse 21, "Submit to one another." This statement is closely linked to the text that follows. Since there is no verb in verse 22, the Greek reader would have taken the verb from the preceding sentence and inserted it. (This is what our translations have done.) This establishes a strong link between verses 21 and 22, showing that verse 21 belongs at the beginning of Paul's teaching on husbands and wives.[87] Thus this often neglected imperative to all believers acts as a qualifier for what Paul is about to say.

Mutual submission erases subservience

The mutual call to submission in Ephesians 5:21 serves to erase any notion of authority and subservience in the section that follows (vv. 22-33). If we ignore the broader imperative of verse 21, we lose the unique message to the husband and wife in this passage. Yes, the wife is enjoined to submit to her husband (v. 22). Yet this does not relieve the husband of his responsibility to do likewise, any more than the command for the husband to love his wife (v. 25) frees the wife from her responsibility to walk in love. As defined earlier, one expression of love is submission.

Sometimes we make distinctions between love and submission, when actually they belong together.[88] One cannot love without giving preference to the one loved. The voluntary surrender of one's rights is the crowning act of love (1 Cor. 13:5; John 12:24).

Too often we interpret Christ-like subordination solely as the wife's duty, while encouraging husbands to dominate. But this is not the biblical picture. If the husband is loving, he will be yielding and will be the first servant of his wife. Thus we must see the word to wives in verse 22 within the framework of mutual submission (vv. 21, 25). That the husband is called to love requires that he adapt himself to his wife (see 1 Cor. 13:4-7).

In 1 Peter 3:1-7, wives are told to submit to their husbands. Sarah's life (vv. 5-6) illustrates this injunction. Sarah deferred to her husband and obeyed him. Some have taken this to mean that submission implies blanket obedience all the time. This is not the case. These verses are merely saying that Sarah's submission took the form of compliance to Abraham's desire.[89] Those who use this argument fail to mention that Abraham also yielded to Sarah and obeyed her (Gen. 21:11-12).

Mutuality, as in Sarah and Abraham

In 1 Peter, the same principle applies as in Ephesians 5. Because the wife receives an instruction to submit as Sarah did does not imply that the husband is not to submit like Abraham did. In fact, verse 7 confirms this conclusion. It says, "Husbands, in the same way be considerate." In what way? In the same way that the wife is to be submissive (v. l) and in the same way that Sarah yielded to Abraham (vv. 5-6), husbands too must behave similarly. In a submissive way they are to be considerate of their wives. Why? Because husbands and wives stand in the same position as "heirs of the gracious gift of life" (v. 7). This common denominator is to affect the way they relate to one another on all levels.

Gilbert Bilezikian comes to a similar conclusion, but includes 1 Peter 2:18-25 in his discussion. He points out that the phrase "in the same manner" connects the three sections (2:18-25; 3:1-6; 3:7). Servants must submit to their masters based on Christ's servant model (2:18-25). "In the same manner" wives are to be submissive (3:1-7). They should adopt the servant attitude modeled by Christ and required by slaves. "In the same manner" husbands are to be considerate (3:7). They should adopt the servant attitude modeled by Christ and required by slaves and wives.[90]

How did Jesus model a submissive role? Cite examples.

Jesus is the prime example for all believers. He modelled servanthood—a submissive role—as the epitome of love. In John 13:1-17, he took the role of a servant by washing his disciples' feet. When he finished, he said, "I have set you an example that you should do as I have done for you" (v. 15). His command, "As I have loved you, so you must love one another" (v. 34) parallels this incident. How had Jesus loved? He loved by becoming a servant to his disciples.

Love demonstrated in servanthood

Again and again, Jesus showed his love through servanthood. He showed the height of this love in his incarnation (John 3:16); he emptied himself and took "the very nature of a servant" (Phil. 2:7). The church's attitude is to reflect this attitude of Christ (Phil. 2:5). Philippians 2:4 explains its practical application: "Each of you should look not only to your own interests, but also to the interests of others." This sums up the "voluntary attitude of giving in" that Christ so richly portrayed.

Meditate on Philippians 2:1-7. List areas in your life where you need to make adjustments. How can you model servant submission in these areas? What are some practical steps you can take to develop a submissive attitude in these situations? Commit yourself to modelling Christ's submissive attitude.

EIGHT

WHO IS IN AUTHORITY?

1 Corinthians 11:2-16; 7:1-5; 1 Timothy 2:12

Several passages of Scripture have been used to support the idea that, based solely on gender, men automatically have authority over women. This has often led the church to ban women from leadership.

Those who hold this tenet pose the question: "How can a woman lead when she cannot, by divine decree, exercise authority over a man?" It can be argued, however, that this perspective places women in a powerless position. It does not allow their decision-making powers to develop. Women may tend to feel less valued than men. And women lose opportunities to mature in many areas. Consequently, the church loses a dimension of wholeness in leadership that carries over into individual families.

This idea can breed inequities in male-female relationships. It can even foster the use of the wrong type of authority: illegitimate and controlling. Thus the challenge for men and women in the church is to reexamine their understanding of related Scriptures.

Look at the following Scriptures and think about how Jesus used authority (Matt. 7:29; Mark 1:22, 27; Matt. 9:6; Luke 4:36; 9:1). What was the outcome?

The life of Jesus is sprinkled with references to his authority (*exousia* and related forms). Amazingly, most of these are used regarding Jesus' ministry acts rather than his right over human lives. In 12 verses, authority (*exousia*) is connected to his teaching; in three verses it is related to his ability to forgive sins; and in another three it is exercised over evil spirits.[91] In these instances, divine authority gave credibility to teaching, enabled healing, and wrought deliverance. It was exercised in service to others.

Jesus' authority was in service, not relationships

Rarely, in the earthly model, did Jesus exercise authority as a commandant, barking orders and demanding compliance. Instead, he led his followers into discipleship. It was through this type of non-dominating influence that he promoted servant-leadership.

Other Scriptures, not fitting in the above categories, are immersed in a redemptive life-giving context. For instance, in Matthew 28:18 Jesus' claim to all authority is immediately joined to a distinct ministry purpose, the discipling of the nations (vv. 19-20). A similar thought is recurrent in John 17:2. The purpose of the Son's authority "over all people" is that he might give them eternal life.

What did Jesus identify as the wrong type of authority (Matt. 20:25-28)? In what ways did he refuse it?

It was this style of authority that Jesus so finely portrayed, a stark contrast to the abusive power structures he condemned. When the multitudes wanted to crown him as an earthly king, he refused. His kingdom operated by different principles. When Peter drew his sword to defend Jesus, Jesus had Peter put the sword away (John 18:10-11). In Luke 9:51-56, on their way to Jerusalem, Jesus' disciples experienced rejection and sought to destroy an entire village. But Jesus rebuked them for their wrong intentions. Jesus' rebuke also came when his disciples were competitive and grasping for position (Matt. 20:20-28).

He turned the organizational chart upside down

By precept and example, Jesus turned the organizational chart upside down, putting the most important at the bottom as servants and bondslaves. "For he who is least among you all—he is the greatest" (Luke 9:48). "The greatest among you will be your servant" (Matt. 23:11). "You know," Jesus said, "that the rulers of the Gentiles lord it over [*katakurieuo*; i.e., control, subjugate] them, and their high officials exercise authority over them. Not so with you. Instead, whoever wants to become great among you must be your servant, and whoever wants to be first must be your slave—just as the Son of Man did not come to be served, but to serve, and to give his life as a ransom for many" (Matt. 20:25-28).

The epistles reiterate this view of authority. Church leaders are not to lord it over (*katakurieuo*) the flock (1 Pet. 5:3). Control and subjugation of church members is forbidden. While Scripture calls Christ Lord (*kurios*, supreme in authority), the church does not share this exalted position.[92] Jesus is called Lord (*kurieuo*, to be lord of, to rule over), but Paul refused to "lord it over" (*kurieuo*) the faith of the Corinthians (2 Cor. 1:24). Instead, he became as a father, a nurse, and a servant to those in his care.

> *What do the epistles say about women's exercise of authority (see 1 Cor. 11:2-16; 7:1-5; 1 Tim. 2:12)? How do these passages seem to affirm or limit that authority? Explain your answers in light of what has been studied so far.*

It is in this light that women's authority should be examined. What does the New Testament specifically say about women and authority?

Paul here deals with a unique situation

A good place to start is 1 Corinthians 11:2-16. It is not clear what led Paul to his discussion in this passage. Yet it is possible that verses 2 through 16 deal with a unique situation in a church that accepted his teaching about the equality of the sexes.[93] Some members may have felt that the head-covering was a denial of this equality, while others possibly feared the outcome of breaking ranks with the social norm.

If this is the case, Paul responds by encouraging them to maintain the covering custom as a sign of the distinction between the sexes. He also assures them that the head-covering does not alter woman's status, but acts as a symbol of her authority and position in Christ. Then he reinforces the interdependence of woman and man and concludes that none of the other churches have abandoned the head-covering practice.[94]

Man is not lord, but source of woman's life

Paul begins his instructions in verse 3: "Now I want you to realize that the head [*kephale*] of every man is Christ, and the head of the woman is man, and the head of Christ is God." Man's authority over woman is not being established in the "head" terminology. As head, man is not lord over woman but the source of her life (i.e., she came from man's rib, Gen. 2:21-22).[95] We find the basis for this conclusion in verse 8: "For man did not come *from* woman, but woman *from* man." The emphasis is upon "the unique relationships that are predicated on one's being the source of the other's existence."[96] This unique relationship implies diversity as well as unity.[97] Thus the stage is set for the remainder of Paul's exhortation in which he targets the diversity (i.e., the gender differences, vv. 4-9) and the unity (vv. 11-12) of the sexes. Sandwiched between these two sections is Paul's statement regarding woman's authority.

Leading up to this statement, Paul emphasizes the distinction between the sexes. In verses 4 through 6 he tells the church to honor the covering custom. The issue is not whether a woman has the right to pray or prophesy publicly; Paul assumes this is taking place.

The issue is how this ministry should be done—with a covered head. When a woman fails to follow this custom, she brings dishonor upon herself.[98] Why? Because the head-covering appears to have been a social symbol of her femaleness.[99] To discard the covering meant a denial of this distinction. If she wants to be like a man, Paul implies, then she should go all the way and shave her head (v. 6).

Woman should not deny her created sexuality

So Paul has no problem with a woman praying and prophesying in the church, but he does have a problem with her doing it in a way that denies her created sexuality, and thus discredits the church.[100]

Then in verses 7 through 9, Paul stresses the creation differences between man and woman based on the Creation accounts. He is now giving a supporting argument for why a woman should have her head covered when praying or prophesying.[101] It is important to remember that Paul's concern is to explain why a woman should follow this covering custom.

Verse 7 says that man is "the image and glory of God, but the woman is the glory of man." Here Paul is not denying that woman is created in God's image, or that she is God's glory also.[102] This is not his point. His point is that woman is the glory of man, something that man can never be. Because woman was taken from man (v. 8) and created for man (v. 9), she is his crowning glory. Without her, he is incomplete.

Woman participates as man's suitable companion

Because woman came from man and is of the same substance, and because she was created for man, she is the one, suitable companion for him. To discard the distinction of the sexes by disregarding the head-covering jeopardizes that relationship, so she ought to wear her head-covering as a sign of her womanhood, an honorable place alongside man. She has authority—with man, yet as a *woman*—to participate in worship (v. 10).

At this point, Paul turns to the woman's authority (v. 10). Here we often understand authority as man's authority over woman.[103] But this interpretation is highly unlikely for at least two reasons. First, "there is no parallel for *exousia* [authority] being used in the passive sense that would be required if this interpretation were correct, and there is nothing in the context to indicate the word was being used in anything but the normal way."[104] Second, the structure of the following verses shows that Paul was referring to woman's authority.

Verse 11 then goes on to say, "In the Lord, however, woman is not independent of man." The order "woman . . . man" makes it almost impossible to interpret the authority in verse 10 as man's authority over woman. If this had been the apostle's intention he probably would have changed the wording to read, "However, man is not independent of woman." Yet this was not done. Paul clearly began, "Woman is not independent of man," distinctly qualifying *her* use of authority.[105]

Man and woman need each other

Verses 11 and 12 not only act as qualifiers for verse 10, they also provide a word of balance. Because woman now has authority does not mean she can do without man. God has orchestrated things so that "in the Lord" man and woman need each other. The picture is one of mutual authority against the backdrop of interrelatedness.

Thus Paul is saying woman has authority (the right and privilege) in the church to pray and prophesy. But her new status in Christ has not erased sexual distinctions. She should exercise her authority and yet maintain her feminine identity. In the Corinthian women's case, this means honoring the covering custom. In this way, the head-covering can become a symbol of their new-found Christian privilege.

Paul also refers to woman's authority in 1 Corinthians 7:1-5. This passage deals with marriage and the conjugal relationship between a husband and wife. In verse 3 a husband and wife must meet each other's needs and expectations: "The husband should fulfill his marital duty to his wife, and likewise the wife to her husband." This involves mutual marital commitment.

Each has authority over the other

Verse 4 then makes this statement: "The wife does not have authority [*exousiazo*] over her own body, but the husband *does*; and likewise also the husband does not have authority [*exousiazo*] over his own body, but the wife *does*" (NASB). Paul is saying that the husband and the wife both have authority over each other. That a wife would have any conjugal rights at all is a surprising claim for Paul's day. Yet Paul states that the right the husband has over his wife exactly parallels her right over him.[106] The husband has authority over his wife, but "likewise," or "in the same way," the wife has this same authority over her husband. Thus not only does marriage involve mutual commitment, it also involves mutual authority.

The sphere of this authority further extends into the realm of decision-making. 1 Corinthians 7:5 says, "Do not deprive each other except by mutual consent." "Mutual consent" means "with one voice." The choice to separate for spiritual reasons *must* be made by mutual agreement. Here Paul portrays decision-making as a shared venture between husband and wife. Paul establishes a possible precedent in this verse; he is presenting a new paradigm. He uses the model of mutual decision-making as an acceptable form within the family nucleus. In fact, the apostle commanded it at this most intimate level between husband and wife.

So we see that authority—as defined by the servanthood of Christ—is equally vested in husband and wife. The husband has authority over his wife, and the wife has authority over her husband. This does not give license to lordship but requires a sensitivity to meet each other's needs (v. 3), to consider each other's personal well-being (v. 4), and to respect one another's decision-making powers (v. 5).

Absolute power can be destructive

We find another important use of authority in 1 Timothy 2:12. Paul said, "I do not permit a woman to teach or to have authority over a man." At first glance, this looks like a blanket prohibition of female leadership contrary to the many examples in Scripture.

However, a closer look at the term shows a prohibition of the exercise of the wrong type of authority. In this verse, the Greek word *authentein* is different from the Greek word translated "authority" in the rest of the New Testament. Here it carries the idea of "a 'self who holds absolute power' over someone or something."[107] The Greeks used it to describe a murderer. While this idea dropped out of use, it still had the "nuance of using such absolute power in a destructive manner, describing the activity of a person who acts for his or her own advantage apart from any consideration of the needs or interests of anyone else."[108]

Thus Paul was forbidding exactly what Jesus forbade when he restrained his disciples from destroying a community in Luke 9 and when he told his disciples not to rule over others like the Gentiles (Matt. 20:25-28). It was the type of "lording over" forbidden by church leaders and rejected by Paul. For further study on this verse, see the next chapter.

> *If you were going to plant a church based on Jesus' model of authority, what would the structure of that church look like? What kind of atmosphere would it have?*
>
> *If you built a church on the "Gentile" model (Matt. 20:25-28), how would it contrast to the first? Which is more biblical? Why?*

NINE

CAN A WOMAN TEACH?

1 Corinthians 14:33-35; 1 Timothy 2:8-15

The Bible expresses a positive attitude toward women in the church and gives examples of women in ministry and of women teaching. Paul's overall instructions reflect this attitude, as does his statement in Galatians 3:28, and his work with women in leadership roles.

Yet when we place this evidence alongside passages like 1 Corinthians 14:33-35 and 1 Timothy 2:8-15, a monumental contradiction seems to appear. Some have ignored this conflict. Some have required women to be silent or have restricted them from teaching. The challenge for the church is to address these difficulties and discover answers that are consistent with the whole counsel of God.

What is the backdrop for interpreting 1 Corinthians 14:33-35 and 1 Timothy 2:8-15?

Throughout the Bible there is evidence of women's participation in teaching, leadership roles, and vocal gifts in the church. Huldah the prophetess probably taught men in the school of prophets (2 Kings 22:14-20).[109] Deborah acted as a leader and prophetess in Israel (Judg. 4:4-7). Miriam, the prophetess and sister of Moses, also had a significant leadership role (Exod. 15:20-21; Mic. 6:4). The women that Paul identified as co-worker, deacon, and apostle must have taught in groups that included men (Phil. 4:2-3; Rom. 16:1-16). Priscilla and her husband taught Apollos, who later became a prominent minister. Many women had vocal participation in the life of the church and some taught (1 Cor. 11:5).

Entire body of Scripture vs. individual passages

These examples, along with the overall biblical view of women, provide the best backdrop for interpreting individual passages of Scripture such as 1 Corinthians 14:33-35 and 1 Timothy 2:8-15. It is a strain on the contextual influence to make these passages the foundation for interpreting the rest of Scripture. The entire body of God's Word should be the foundation for interpreting individual passages. This is especially true since these passages deal with particular, cultural problems.

What main problem was Paul dealing with in 1 Corinthians 14? How does this help your understanding of verses 33-35?

The women in the Corinthian church came from a cultic background known for its noisy religious expressions. These expressions included shouting, savagery, and other types of excessive behavior of which the women were a prominent part. It seems inconceivable that this background would not have influenced the recent Corinthian converts.[110]

Obviously, the situation in 1 Corinthians 14 was missing the control of the Holy Spirit.[111] People were speaking out of turn and disrupting the service. There was confusion and, therefore, a need for divine order and peace. Self-control was necessary in the midst of spontaneity and freedom of expression.

It was in this context that Paul asked the women to control their excessive exuberance. In view of the disruption, he declared, "Women should remain silent in the churches. They are not allowed to speak, but must be in submission, as the Law says" (1 Cor. 14:34).

Is this a contradiction?

This statement presents a blatant contradiction to Scripture if we understand it as a command for total silence by *all* women in *all* churches. It conflicts with Paul's earlier assumption that women will pray and prophesy (1 Cor. 11:5, 13). There is nothing to suggest that the speaking in 11:5 occurs in a private meeting or involves different people than those addressed in chapter 14. Paul had openly accepted women's vocal ministry providing they were properly attired.

We also should remember that there were women prophets in the church (Acts 21:9). Furthermore, if 1 Corinthians 14:34 is an absolute prohibition, then we must understand the entire chapter (possibly even chapters 12-14) to exclude women.[112] Yet such a conclusion is improbable.[113]

One way of dealing with the problems raised in this text is to see verses 34 and 35 as a prohibition against a specific abuse within the church.[114]

Consider this vignette. The women at Corinth wanted to learn, a privilege historically denied them.[115] But they were pursuing their desire in an inappropriate way that was disrupting the order of the service. Paul did not stop them in their pursuit, but redirected them instead. "If they want to inquire [learn (NASB)] about something," he instructed, "they should ask their own husbands at home . . ." Otherwise, they "should remain silent in the churches." They should not be disrupting the service with their inquiries. Whatever the specific situation may have been, it was serious enough to warrant direct, corrective measures by the apostle.

"Silence" was also enjoined for prophets

Several other observations are in order. While the silence (*sigao*) enjoined by Paul in verse 34 refers to absolute silence, verses 28 and 30 used it of tongue speakers and prophets. This implies that the silence expected of women is not absolute anymore than it was absolute for the prophets.[116] In the interest of peace and order, Paul commanded the women to be silent, just as he would have commanded a male prophet to be silent if his speech was disruptive or unedifying.[117]

To the entire church, men and women, Paul penned, "When you come together, *everyone* has a hymn, or a word of instruction, a revelation, a tongue or an interpretation" (v. 26). A few verses later he continued, "You can *all* prophesy" (v. 31). On this basis, it hardly seems that Paul disapproved of women's vocal contribution in worship and discussion.

Paul uses the word "submission"in verse 34 in an unusual way. Whenever the verb "submit" appears elsewhere in the New Testament, a statement usually accompanies it indicating to whom one is to submit.[118] Here women are told to be in submission but not to whom. This unusual construction may suggest that Paul is asking the women to submit to the order of the service, or merely to adopt a submissive attitude.[119] It is also worth noting that the apostle uses a form of the same word when speaking of the prophets in verse 32. This suggests that Paul asked both the women and the prophets to do the same thing: adopt an attitude conducive to a peaceful atmosphere and an orderly meeting.[120]

"As the Law says"

Paul said of the women, "They must be in submission, as the Law says" (v. 34). What "law" was Paul referring to? There are at least two possible interpretations posited by scholars. Some scholars suggest Paul was appealing to Scripture.[121] However, there is no single text requiring female submission in either the Mosaic Law or anywhere else in the Old Testament. While it is possible that Paul was referring to some sense of this prohibition in the Old Testament, it is difficult to find any passage resembling his instructions.[122]

Another possible interpretation is that Paul was appealing to general Jewish or Gentile laws. There were many restrictions placed on women in the rabbinic tradition. "Seen in this way, Paul is not exalting rabbinic tradition as an ultimate authority but using law generally as representative of general restrictions placed on women in first-century society."[123]

Besides the Jewish prohibitions, there were many Greek and Roman laws used to control the ecstatic outbursts and activities of women in various cultic services. It seems that extensive legal efforts were made to control this behavior.[124] Accordingly, Paul's concern that society should not discredit the church compelled him to issue his statement. While it is true that he never used "law" in this way previously, this interpretation considers the apostle's sensitivity to social propriety.

Self-control was called for

Whichever interpretation one chooses, the point is there was an authority validating Paul's exhortation. To conclude that this exhortation means acquiescence or total silence, however, is not necessary. For the sake of local church order, Paul asked the women to exercise self-control, based on the reasonableness of the "law."

Paul was not demanding total silence of these women anymore than he was of the rest of the church. He was appealing for self-control and decorum, which would preserve the spontaneity and unity of church life. This group of uneducated, Christian women wanted to learn. But to learn, not only must they put away disruptive behavior, they also must control their eager inquiries and discuss their questions at home (v. 35).

What prohibitions did Paul seem to place on women in 1 Timothy 2:8-15? How do they conflict with other Bible teachings and examples?

1 Timothy 2:8-15 also addresses the way in which women participate in the worship service. Verses 8 through 10 begin by discussing how men and women are to pray when they gather together.[125] Men are to "lift up holy hands in prayer, without anger or disputing." Women should pray dressed in attire that will not draw undue attention to themselves. Paul's concern here, as with the Corinthian church, was with decency and propriety. Prayer should be made in the right spirit and in

a way that will not be distracting or disruptive. Paul then turns to the issue of learning (vv. 11-15).

At Ephesus, there was a heretical onslaught

To understand the intention of Paul's instruction about women in the following verses, it is important to see what he was dealing with. At Ephesus, there was a heretical onslaught, an inroad of erroneous teaching that threatened the life of the church.[126] One of Paul's combative measures was to remove and restrain all unqualified teachers (1 Tim. 1:3; 6:3-5; cf. Titus 1:10-11). Since women at this time were uneducated, they were prime targets for heresy and ill-equipped to teach.

Yet restraining unqualified teachers was not enough. Vigorous, sound teaching was in order (1 Tim. 4:11; 2 Tim. 2:25; 4:2; Titus 2:1). Reliable people, including older men and women, were to be taught so that they might instruct others (2 Tim. 2:2; Titus 2:1-5). Since women in general were uneducated, they also needed to be taught. For this to happen, they had to adopt a learning posture (1 Tim. 2:11).

Thus Paul's emphasis falls upon learning (vv. 11-15). The Ephesian women were untaught. Education usually was not a privilege they shared in the Graeco-Roman world.[127] Judaism, out of which Paul came, forbade women to teach, did not permit them to bear witness, and generally did not allow them to receive instruction.[128]

In this light, Paul's encouragement for the women to learn is revolutionary. Here was a man steeped in Jewish tradition, directing the women to participate as pupils. They wanted to teach, but had not yet been taught. Paul's answer to their dilemma was, "Learn."

He then proceeds to explain how they are to learn. Adopting a learning posture requires an appropriate attitude. This attitude includes quietness and submissiveness (v. 11).[129] A woman cannot learn if she does not listen and yield to the instructor.

Verse 12 follows the learning injunction: "I do not permit a woman to teach or to have authority over a man; she must be silent." This is the posture she must adopt while learning. However, some have understood this as an absolute prohibition against women teaching men. To argue, as some do, that the teaching refers to official teaching in the church body as opposed to general one-on-one instruction seems unwarranted and almost impossible to apply. Distinctions between "official" and "non-official" teaching are difficult to substantiate in the New Testament.[130]

Others claim that a woman cannot teach because she cannot exercise authority over man. But to say that a woman can never have authority over a man is a denial of Paul's statement to the contrary. As previously noted, 1 Corinthians 7:4 clearly states, "The husband does not have authority [*exousiazo*] over his own body, but the wife *does*" (NASB). To restrict the authority in verse 12 to the teaching function sidesteps 1 Corinthians 7:4 but raises another problem. Teaching is not viewed as a necessarily authoritative function in the New Testament.[131] The Bible seems to apply greater status and authority to prophesying, something the Corinthian women did (1 Cor. 11:5). Thus, instead of viewing verse 12 as an absolute prohibition, it seems best to interpret it as a temporary, local restriction.

This makes sense upon closer inspection. The phrase, "I do not permit" (v. 12) may imply the temporary nature of the restriction. It is possible that Paul's use of "I do not permit," instead of the more formal, "It is not permitted," shows he is using his personal judgment to say women should not teach at the present time.[132]

Believers are not to be domineering people

The word used for authority (*authentein*) also implies unusual circumstances. Verse 12 is the only place in the New Testament where this word occurs. It means "to lord it over."[133] Paul was forbidding the Ephesian women to exercise dominating control over the men. It was this type of behavior that Jesus' disciples were forbidden to exercise (Matt. 20:25-26) and Paul himself rejected (2 Cor. 1:24). What Paul required of these women was no different from what is required of any believer. Believers must not be domineering people.

Paul then proceeds to illustrate his point in verses 13 and 14. Some people use these verses as an argument to show why it is improper for a woman to teach a man. They argue that verse 13 establishes man's (Adam's) priority over woman (Eve); woman should not teach because she is subordinate. They also use verse 14 to reason that woman is easily deceived and thus cannot be trusted to teach. Neither of these positions is ultimately defensible.

First, to assume that man is superior because God created him first is not a necessary conclusion. The New Testament never makes this inference, nor does Genesis. That God created woman second is not a strong argument favoring her subjection.[134] Being first does not mean being the best, not in the contemporary vernacular nor in God's economy.

In making his statement in verse 13, Paul possibly established a loose parallel between the men and women in the Ephesian church (v. 12) and Adam and Eve (v. 13). As God created Adam first, so the men at Ephesus were taught first; they already had the skills necessary to teach. This was not a negative reflection on the women because just as Eve was physically formed, they would be spiritually formed and shaped as they learned.

Second, to argue that women cannot teach men because they are easily deceived is inconsistent with the fact that the church permits them to teach other women and children (2 Tim. 1:5; 3:14-15; Titus 2:3-4).[135] If women are easily deceived and unable to discern truth, then why did Paul allow them to teach at all? If Paul intended this interpretation, then he would not have allowed the women to infect *anyone* in the church— particularly future generations—with wrong teaching.

The entire Corinthian church is compared to Eve

The apostle was not saying that women are generally more prone to deception than men. In 2 Corinthians 11:3, he compared the entire Corinthian church, male and female, to

Eve in her deception.[136] It would be ridiculous, based on this verse in 2 Corinthians, to conclude that *all* believers are easily deceived. It is equally ridiculous, based on 1 Timothy 2:14, to conclude that *all* women are easily deceived. Any person is susceptible to error when ignorant of God's Word. Thus it would be better to draw a more specific parallel between Eve in her deception and the unique situation regarding the women at Ephesus.

The Ephesian women were not rooted and established in God. While they remained ignorant of God's ways, they could not teach others. Later, however, when they matured and no longer resembled Eve in her vulnerable moment, they would eventually be qualified to teach.

Again, this ban on women teaching was not final. Verse 15 says, "Women will be kept safe [saved] through childbirth, if they continue in faith, love and holiness with propriety." The word "women" in this sentence is singular in the Greek text. So this part of the verse should read, "Woman will be saved through childbirth." While a singular subject is used here, the second part of the verse uses a plural subject translated as "they." What does this mean?[137]

A possible explanation is that Paul is using the term "woman" collectively. The idea is that woman, or womankind, as represented by Eve, would be saved from the theological implications of the fall through childbearing.[138] In what ways? First, it would be through woman that the effects of the Fall would be reversed. At the time Eve transgressed, God gave the promise of redemption through her seed (Gen. 3:15). She would bear the seed of the Messiah who was to bring redemption and eradicate the effects of the Fall.[139]

Eve was honored as the mother of all living

Second, it would be through woman that all subsequent generations would be birthed. In Genesis 3:20, Adam honored Eve as the mother of all living. Although she had been an instrument of sin and death in the Fall, she would become an instrument of salvation and life.

As woman (in general) would be saved from the implications of the Fall through childbearing, the Ephesian women, specifically, would be saved from their current condition of having their teaching prohibited if they would continue "in faith, love, and holiness" (v. 15). A deliverance similar to Eve's was available for them. For it was their failure to "continue in faith," and not their femaleness, that required their silence.[140]

Salvation (or wholeness) would come through a process of learning in quietness and submission (v. 11). When the marks of maturity (steadfastness in faith, love, and holiness) became evident, they could then teach.[141]

Paul was not banning women from teaching because of their gender. He forbade untaught women from teaching, just as he forbade "certain men not to teach false doctrines any longer" (1 Tim. 1:3). (Also see Titus 1:10-11 where Paul demanded that troublemakers be silenced.) If women, by nature, were prone to deception, then why did Paul encourage and endorse women teachers elsewhere (Titus 2:3)?

No, Paul was not censoring female teachers. He was forbidding the ill-equipped from exercising illegitimate authority and from possibly poisoning the church with further erroneous doctrine. His answer to this problem was that these Ephesian women should learn with an attitude of receptivity (v. 11) so that they might be saved into ecclesiastical wholeness (v. 15), and thus teach from a position of maturity.

Imagine yourself in either the Corinthian church or the Ephesian church. You are a first-time visitor prior to Paul's letters to them. Describe the activities in the service. Include things that surprise you, elements that you find distasteful, and aspects that are pleasing to you.

After the service, you have the opportunity to converse with several members of the congregation. What is your impression of them? They also want to know your impressions of their church. Jot them down.

How do the messages in these two passages apply to you?

TEN

SHOULD WOMEN BE LEADERS?

1 Corinthians 12; Romans 16:1-4, 7; 1 Timothy 3:1-13

In modern "Western" society there has been an upsurge of women in dynamic and prominent roles. Women have seen new horizons in careers and have reached out to develop and exercise their abilities. This social move, with a new awareness of spiritual giftings, has brought the church face to face with the topic of women in leadership. Thus the church is forced to deal with the issue.[142] The challenge is to reevaluate Scripture to determine whether female leadership is the move of God or merely another example of the world's social trends invading the church.

Consider 1 Corinthians 12. What does it reveal about the church? Are there any restrictions placed on women's function in the body of Christ?

In approaching the issue of women as leaders, 1 Corinthians 12 makes a good launching pad. The entire chapter focuses on the importance of the effective functioning of each member in the body of Christ. This chapter clearly shows that racial, social, or sexual distinctions do not determine the distribution of divine gifts. The sole qualification is baptism into Christ's body (v. 13). "There are different kinds of service, but the same Lord. There are different kinds of working, but the same God works all of them in all men" (vv. 5-6). Then the Holy Spirit displays God's power through *each* member to help the entire church. Verses 8 through 11 list some of these special abilities, and verse 28 presents others, especially the leadership abilities. In all this, the concern is proper adaptation in the church and acceptance of gifts in fellow believers.

Women in leadership often face folded arms

However, it appears that when God imparts his grace upon a woman for leadership duties, she often meets with folded arms and "spiritually" clenched fists. She hears the words "I don't need you" (1 Cor. 12:21), which are contrary to God's design. As a result, when "one part suffers, every part suffers with it" (1 Cor. 12:26). We conclude that the church has suffered because it has cut off many of its female members who belong in leadership roles. Thus, in a sense, God himself was cut off from full expression within the church and the world.

What are some arguments against women in leadership? Can you review them? In light of what has been studied so far, how are these arguments nullified?

A brief look at the arguments against women as leaders will help clear the air for a fresh view of the issue. Opponents say that while men and women are equal, women are functionally subordinate, and thus cannot assume leadership roles. This subordination is based on a "chain of command" (a hierarchy) that was established at creation and cannot be broken. The glue that holds this hierarchy together is authority (based on an erroneous view of headship), which the church sees as its backbone. On top of this, Scripture supposedly places additional restrictions on women: they must be silent in the church (1 Cor. 14:34), and must not teach or have authority over a man (1 Tim. 2:12).

However, the evidence barring women from leadership has loopholes. Female subordination based on Adam's prior creation is ill-founded. Adam's creation prior to Eve does not prove his authority over her any more than the prior creation of the birds gave them authority over Adam. Eve's creation from Adam's rib did not make her subordinate; it showed that she was of the same substance. After all, we never consider Adam subordinate to the dirt from which he was fashioned.

The statement in Genesis 3 about the husband ruling his wife was an acknowledgement of what would happen because of sin, not a license for husbands to dominate. The ground was equally cursed with thorns and thistles (Gen. 3:17-18), but this has not stopped people from diligently combating the encroachment of weeds in their lawns and flowerbeds.[143] If Christians fight the curse of thorns and thistles, they have the duty continually to combat the erosive effects of the sin of domination.

Christian authority is not lordship but servanthood

The figurative use of "head" refers to one who is the life-source of another. As head of his wife, the husband is the source of her life, growth, and nurture. There is *no* hint of authority or rulership in this word. Scripture does not define authority within the body of Christ in terms of lordship. In the church, it is always perceived in the context of servanthood. In the husband-wife relationship, servanthood is expressed in mutual submission. Both voluntarily give in and cooperate, deferring to the other. Wives should submit to their husbands, and husbands should submit to their wives as an act of love (Eph. 5:21-33).

While Paul told women in particular instances to be quiet (1 Cor. 14:34), at other times he told them to speak (1 Cor. 11:5). Sometimes they were forbidden to teach, especially when they were unqualified, unstable, untaught, and immature (1 Tim. 2:11-15). This evidence points toward a positive role for women in ministry and in no way prevents them from being leaders.

What type of leadership roles did women in the early church

*exercise? Identify specific women and think about how they
are described or addressed in Scripture.*

In Romans 16:1, Paul calls Phoebe "a servant [*diakonos*] of
the church in Cenchrea." *Diakonos* means "servant" or "minister" and is sometimes translated "deacon" in the New Testament. Paul used this word for Christ, Apollos, Epaphras,
Timothy, and himself.[144] In these cases, Paul linked it with
ministry activities, which sometimes included preaching and
teaching. There is no valid reason to think this term carries any
less weight when applied to Phoebe than it does when used of
Paul, Apollos, Timothy, or Tychicus. When referring to these
men, most versions translate *diakonos* as "minister."

Paul applies the same word to Phoebe, and it is best
translated, as it is of other people in the epistles, as "minister"
or "deacon."[145] Calling Phoebe a *diakonos of the church* reinforces this conclusion. Her activity in this regard was directly
associated with the church. This suggests she had a specific
ministry within the congregation at Cenchrea.[146] There is no
reason to suppose that the service rendered by her in this
capacity was any different from that of Paul and his fellow
workers.[147]

Phoebe was a steward, a manager

Paul also greeted Phoebe as a "help to many" (Rom.
16:2). The term "help" is a weak translation of *prostatis*, which
means "protectress" or "patron."[148] Its masculine form in the
LXX is used of stewards (1 Chron. 27:31), officers (1 Chron.
29:6), chief officers (2 Chron. 24:11), and other leaders.[149] In the
New Testament, its verb form is translated "govern" (Rom.
12:8), "are over" (1 Thess. 5:12), "manage" (1 Tim. 3:4-5, 12),
and "direct" (1 Tim. 5:17). In each of these cases, the word is
descriptive of a leader or the activity of a leader.

A look at New Testament passages on church leadership
reveals an intimate relationship between caring and govern-
ing. Caring for and watching over the flock are chief functions
of those in charge of the church. Thus the word *prostatis* sug-

gests a significant role in the church. It suggests one who is entrusted with watching over the flock. And it does not seem necessary to limit this role to a physical form of assistance, although this may have been the author's point if the sense of a patron was intended. As a protectress of the church, Phoebe have functioned in a pastoral capacity. Thus, whether as a patron, protectress, or both, Phoebe was a prominent woman of authority and responsibility.[150]

Some would refuse to accept this conclusion, objecting that such a claim would place Paul in a subordinate position to Phoebe. After all, they would argue, she was a *prostatis* to many people, including Paul (Rom. 16:2). However, it is hard to believe that Paul never submitted himself to other church leaders. Nor is there evidence he considered himself on a higher level than they.

But whether Paul was ever subordinate to Phoebe is not the issue. The point is that Phoebe, somewhere along the line, offered Paul leadership, care and assistance for which he was grateful. This does not need to mean anything more than partnership in the ministry of the gospel.

Junia was known as an apostle

Paul designated another female leader, Junia in Romans 16:7, as "outstanding among the apostles." This name has been translated by some as Junia (female) and by others as Junias (male). Many commentators prefer the masculine spelling (Junias) as a contraction of Junianus. The difficulty with this preference, however, is that we cannot find the masculine form elsewhere.[151] On the other hand, Junia (the feminine form) was a very common Roman name for a woman and is the most natural reading.[152] Furthermore, Chrysostom, a fourth-century church theologian, spoke highly of Junia as a woman apostle.[153] Why then do some scholars insist on the masculine spelling?

The crux of the problem lies with the inability of these scholars to accept the presence of a female apostle in the early church. We can best understand "outstanding among the apostles" as "notable in the ranks of the apostles" rather than "well known to the apostles."[154]

Thus, if we accept the feminine, Junia, this means the early church had at least one female apostle, an unacceptable thought for some. James Dunn addresses this problem in a straightforward manner: "The assumption that it must be male is a striking indictment of male presumption regarding the character and structure of earliest Christianity."[155]

While there is no evidence that women were elders in the early church, there is also no evidence that they were restricted from this position. We find much of our information on elders in 1 Timothy 3. Verses 1 through 7 discuss the qualifications for these overseers. The qualification that an overseer must be "the husband of one wife" does not necessarily limit the office to a married man. Because of Paul's positive teaching on the single state in 1 Corinthians 7, it seems best to understand this to mean that the elders at that time and place were men, and these men happened to be married. Paul was saying that when a male elder is a married man, he must be the husband of one wife. He gives no cause to assume that an elder must always be male and married.

Was Paul referring to deacons' wives?

Paul then goes on to discuss female deacons in 1 Timothy 3:11. While some have identified these women as deacons' wives, evidence favors calling them deacons. In this verse, because there is no article with the noun "women" suggests that the elders, deacons, and women in the chapter represent specific categories of service.[156] The repetition of "likewise" in verses 8 and 11 (NASB) further reinforces this suggestion.

The author is conveying the idea of a list in a series of similar categories. The transitional word "likewise" in verse 11 would lead the reader to expect a new and yet similar grouping to that of the elders and deacons mentioned in verses 1 through 10.[157] Paul is establishing a parallel that he further strengthens by the list of nearly identical qualities expected of the deacons (vv. 8-10) and the women (v. 11). The idea is that the elders should meet certain qualifications; likewise, the deacons should meet similar qualifications. As elders and deacons should measure up, so too should women.

But not all women are the subject of concern here. Paul would not make a general reference to women of the congregation in the middle of a list of special groups.[158] Is it possible then that Paul was referring to deacons' wives? Probably not. Had he meant the wives of church leaders it seems he would have included the article or possessive pronoun to identify the women as "their wives." But the article or pronoun is missing.

Also, it would have been unusual for Paul to discuss deacons' wives but not the wives of the elders. If there were requirements for one group, why not the other?

Finally, it is clear elsewhere that there were women deacons. Since this title (*diakonos*) is used to identify both men and women, there is no reason to suppose women deacons functioned differently from their male counterparts.[159] Thus the evidence favors interpreting the women in verse 11 as female deacons, a special leadership group in addition to the elders and male deacons.

Titus 2:3 refers to older women (*presbutidas*). These women were to be trained to teach "what is good." Although their teaching was to include training the younger women (Titus 2:4), it cannot be deduced that the church limited this teaching to women. These older women were to take leadership in training others.

Women who contended on behalf of the gospel

Another word describing a ministerial office is *sunergos*, meaning "fellow workers."[160] It is used of Paul, Timothy, Titus, Epaphroditus, Mark, Luke, Priscilla (Rom. 16:3), and two women, Euodia and Syntyche, who contended with Paul on behalf of the gospel (Phil. 4:2-3). In describing these people as fellow workers, Paul was identifying them as significant individuals in the cause of the kingdom. In addition, Paul's description of Euodia and Syntyche in Philippians 4:2-3 implies that they had authority in the church.

Finally, in 1 Timothy 5:14, Paul counseled "younger widows to marry, to have children, to manage their homes, and to give the enemy no opportunity for slander." He was instructing these women to take leadership responsibility in their homes. "Manage" (*oikodespoteo*) means to "rule a family, to rule over the house, to be master of the house."[161] They were to rule the affairs of the household of which their new husbands would be a part. Paul also told the elders (who were probably male at that time) and male deacons to manage (*proistemi*) their households (1 Tim. 3:4, 12). From this combination of verses it appears that Paul expected joint leadership of both the man and the woman in the home.

Considering this overview and specific evidence, "Should women be leaders?" does not seem to be the appropriate question. The appropriate question is, "Will the church allow women to be what God has already ordained them to be?"

> *Imagine that you are talking to a young woman who desires to pastor a church. She explains that God has called her to do so. Several people have told her it is unscriptural for her to aspire to this role. She must not rule over a man and can only pastor if supervised by a man. What might you say to encourage and affirm the validity of her call? Be sure to include Scriptures to verify your points.*

Review Questions

1. Discuss the commonly understood meaning of "head." Do you think this is the biblical meaning? Why?

2. What were some functions of Christ's headship? (Consider Eph. 1:22-23; 4:15-16; 5:21-33; Col. 1:15-20; 2:19.)

3. In what sense is man head of woman? Husband head of his wife? Consider Jesus' example of headship.

4. What does submission mean? List some of its synonyms and antonyms.

5. Think about mutual submission. Is it appropriate in the church? The home? How would it affect relationships in these areas?

6. How did Jesus model a submissive role? Cite examples.

7. Look at some of the following Scriptures and think about how Jesus used authority (Matt. 7:29; Mark 1:22, 27; Matt. 9:6; Luke 4:36; 9:1). What was the outcome?

8. What did Jesus identify as the wrong type of authority (Matt. 20:25-28)? In what ways did he refuse it?

9. What do the epistles say about women's exercise of authority (see 1 Cor. 11:2-16; 7:1-5; 1 Tim. 2:12)? How do these passages seem to affirm or limit that authority? Explain your answers in light of what has been studied so far.

10. What is the best backdrop for interpreting 1 Corinthians 14:33-35 and 1 Timothy 2:8-15?

11. What main problem was Paul dealing with in 1 Corinthians 14? How does this help your understanding of verses 33-35?

12. What prohibitions did Paul seem to place on women in 1 Timothy 2:8-15? How do these conflict with other Bible teachings and examples?

13. Consider 1 Corinthians 12. What does it reveal about the church? Are there any restrictions placed on women's function in the body of Christ?

14. What are some arguments against women as leaders? In light of what has been studied so far, how are these arguments nullified?

15. What type of leadership roles did women in the early church exercise? Identify specific women and discuss how they are described or addressed in Scripture.

NOTES

1. Paul King Jewett, *The Ordination of Women* (Grand Rapids: Wm. B. Eerdmans Pub. Co., 1980), pp. 27, 29.

2. Mary J. Evans, *Woman In the Bible* (Downers Grove: InterVarsity Press, 1983), p.21.

3. Stephen James M. Brown, *Image and Truth: Studies in the Imagery of the Bible* (Rome: Catholic Book Agency, 1955), p.45.

4. Ibid.

5. Ibid.

6. Ibid.

7. George Bradford Caird, *The Language and Imagery of the Bible* (Philadelphia: The Westminster Press, 1980), p. 174.

8. Jewett, *Ordination*, p. 43.

9. Ibid., p.45.

10. Ibid., pp. 46, 47.

11. Ludwig Hugo Köhler, *Old Testament Theology*, A.S. Todd, trans., (Philadelphia: The Westminster Press, 1957), pp.21, 22.

12. Leonard J. Swidler, *Biblical Affirmations of Women* (Philadelphia: The Westminster Press, 1979), p. 33.

13. Dr. Gordon McConville, consultant to the Women's Commission at World Vision International, Notes, December 1991, World Vision Great Britain, Northampton.

14. Vinay Samuel observes that there is no conscious attempt in Scripture to emphasize the humanity of Jesus above his masculinity, but does acknowledge that Jesus came as the "last Adam" representative of humanity. Samuel was a consultant to the Women's Commission at World Vision International, Notes, December 1991, World Vision Great Britain, Northampton.

15. Joachim Jeremias, "*anthropos*," in *The Theological Dictionary of the New Testament*, abridged in one volume by Geoffrey W. Bromiley (Grand Rapids and Devon: Wm. B. Eerdmans Pub. Co. and The Paternoster Press Ltd., 1985), pp. 59, 60; A. Oepke, "*aner*," in *The Theological Dictionary of the New Testament*, abridged in one volume by Geoffrey W. Bromiley (Grand Rapids and Devon: Wm. B. Eerdmans Pub. Co. and The Paternoster Press Ltd., 1985), p.59.

16. Sheila D. Collins, *A Different Heaven and Earth* (Valley Forge: Judson Press, 1974), p.67.

17. Ibid., p. 66.

18. *Webster's Third New International Dictionary*, s.v. "inferior."

19. Ibid.

20. Some scholars claim that there is no contention between equality and hierarchy. This could be true if potential for "moving up the ladder" exists. If, however, this potential is withheld on the basis of an inherent quality, such as gender or race, then the statement becomes invalid.

    The author agrees with Jack Rogers' statement in his rebuttal in the Kenyon Case:

    > The fallacy is that one cannot be both subordinate *and* equal unless that subordination is voluntary. I have an associate on my church staff who is subordinate to me. But there is nothing to prevent him from becoming the senior pastor. The flaw in the argument of Kenyon and others is that they claim there is something inherently subordinate about women in God's law or the law of nature. That kind of inherent subordination is not compatible with equality. ("The Kenyon Case," *Women and Men in Ministry: Collected Readings*, Roberta Hestenes, comp. [Pasadena: Fuller Theological Seminary, 1988], p. 325.)

21. Paul King Jewett, *Man as Male and Female* (Grand Rapids: Wm. B. Eerdmans Pub. Co., 1975), p.131.

22. The author is not identifying the "image of God" in man as the mutual relationship between man and woman, as Paul Jewett does. It is not my intention to enter into this discussion here. *The New International Dictionary of New Testament Theology*, edited by Colin Brown, is a helpful resource for those desiring to study this issue in depth.

23. Aida Besancon Spencer, *Beyond the Curse* (Nashville: Thomas Nelson Publishers, 1985), p. 21.

24. Julie Renner provides this insight. She translates the text, "God created humankind in his image in the image of God he created

them; male and female he created them." She suggests that the argument based on unity is unnecessary when the text is thus translated. (Notes provided by Julie Renner, consultant to the Women's Commission at World Vision International, November 1991, World Vision Great Britain, Northampton.)

25. Gary Smalley and John Trent, *The Blessing* (Nashville: Thomas Nelson Publishers, 1986), pp. 24-29.

26. The Hebrew text in verse 28 makes it clear that both man and woman received God's blessing as well as his instructions to be fruitful, to subdue the earth, and to rule earth's creatures.

27. William Wilson, *New Wilson's Old Testament Word Studies* (Grand Rapids: Kregal Publications, 1987), p. 215.

28. Out of 21 Old Testament references to "help" (*ezer*), 16 are used of God (Exod. 18:4; Deut. 33:7, 26, 29; Ps. 20:2; 33:20; 70:5; 89:19; 115:9-11; 121:1-2; 124:8; 146:5; Hos. 13:9). Of the remaining five references, two are used of woman as man's "help" (Gen. 2:18, 20), and the remaining three refer to the help or aid given to a weakened, failing army or people (Isa. 30:5; Ezek. 12:14; Dan. 11:34). (George V. Wigram, *The New Englishman's Hebrew Concordance* [Peabody, Mass.: Hendrickson Pub., Inc., 1984], p. 918.)

29. Gilbert Bilezikian points out that the Hebrew language has four other terms for "helper" denoting submission. None of these are used here. (*Beyond Sex Roles* [Grand Rapids: Baker Book House, 1986], p. 217). If the author's intention was to communicate the subordinate role of woman, certainly one of these four would have been used. Paul K. Jewett further claims that this word is "never used elsewhere to designate a subordinate." (*Male and Female*, p. 124.)

30. F. Delitzsch translates "suitable help" as "help of his like;" Claus Westermann translates as "that which is over against, counterpart," and Jewett translates as "corresponding to," "equal and adequate." (C. F. Keil and F. Delitzsch, "The Pentateuch," *Biblical Commentary on the Old Testament*, Vol. 1, James Martin, trans., [Edinburgh: T. & T. Clark, 1864], p. 86; Claus Westermann, *Genesis 1-11: A Commentary*, John J. Scullion, S.J., trans., [Minneapolis: Augsburg Pub. House, 1984], p. 227; Jewett, *Male and Female*, p. 124.) Leonard J. Swidler adds further insight: "The word *neged* [suitable] adjoining *ezer* indicates equality, meaning literally 'alongside of.'" (*Biblical Affirmations of Women*, p. 78.)

31. Westermann, pp. 228-232.

32. Nahum M. Sarna, "Genesis," *The J. P. S. Torah Commentary*, Vol. 2

(Philadelphia: The Jewish Publication Society, 1989), p. 23.

33. Swidler, p. 76.

34. Westermann indicates that this is a "formula of relationship" such as is found in Genesis 29:14; Judges 9:2-3; 2 Samuel 5:1; 19:13-14. He points out that each of these cases refers to a permanent relationship, p. 232.

35. Jewett, *Male and Female*, p. 67.

36. Letha Scanzoni and Nancy Hardesty, *All We're Meant to Be* (Waco: Word Books Pub., 1974), p. 32.

37. E. Margaret Howe, *Women and Church Leadership* (Grand Rapids: Zondervan Pub. House, 1982), p. 50.

38. Evans, p. 17.

39. Sarna, p. 25.

40. Ibid.

41. Shirley F. Bentall contributes the following insight: These "verbs [in Gen. 3:16] which have been translated, traditionally in the future imperative, as if they were commands, were actually written in the simple future tense of Hebrew, and should be interpreted as God's statement or forecast of what would happen as a result of the Fall . . ., not as his eternal punishment upon woman." (From "What Does God's Word Say to Women Today?," an unpublished paper for the Baptist Women of the Alberta Area, 1983, p. 4; cf. Swidler, p. 80.) In a consultation with Dr. McConville, he indicated that one cannot conclude an imperative meaning based on the Hebrew tense alone.

42. Bilezikian favors the first option (*Sex Roles*, p. 55). The second option is a possibility based on the use of the same word, "desire," to describe sin's dominating aims in Genesis 4:7.

43. It is not the author's intention to ignore the impact of community and the sense of community being developed in these early chapters of Genesis. The point in issue is that man and woman each made individual decisions regardless of other influences. It was this personal choice, and the attending action, that determined their guilt. In 3:9, God did not address both man and woman, he spoke directly to man. Likewise in 3:13, God addressed the woman, confronting her with her sin, not that of her husband.

44. Barbara J. MacHaffie, *Her Story* (Philadelphia: Fortress Press, 1986), pp. 24, 25.

45. Evans, pp. 32, 34, 39, 41.

46. Scanzoni, p. 59.

47. Joachim Jeremias, *Jerusalem in the Time of Jesus* (Philadelphia: Fortress Press, 1969), pp. 360, 374, 375.

48. Jeremias quotes CA 2.201 to verify his point: "The woman, says the Law, is in all things inferior to man." (p. 375)

49. Ibid., p. 367.

50. Dorothy Sayers, *Are Women Human?* (Grand Rapids: Wm. B. Eerdmans Pub. Co., 1971), p. 46.

51. MacHaffie, p. 16.

52. Swidler, pp. 164, 165.

53. Evans observes that "the women who followed Jesus showed a greater perseverance, a greater loyalty and possibly a greater faith than even the twelve apostles." She also adds that there is no record of women ever opposing Jesus (pp. 55, 57).

54. Jewett, *Male and Female*, p. 99.

55. Sayers, p. 47.

56. John Norman Davidson Kelly, "A Commentary on the Pastoral Epistles," *Harper's New Testament Commentaries*, Vol. 13 (New York and Evanston: Harper & Row, Pub., 1963), p. 83; Don Williams, *The Apostle Paul and Women in the Church* (Van Nuys: Bim Pub. Co., 1977), pp. 46-119.

57. William Hendriksen, "Exposition of Galatians," *New Testament Commentary*, Vol. 9 (Grand Rapids: Baker Book House, 1968), p. 149; Marvin Richardson Vincent, *Word Studies in the New Testament*, Vol. IV (New York: Charles Scribner's Sons, 1914), p. 129.

58. In Jewish prayers and Greek proverbs the differences between the three categories (Jew-Greek; slave-free; male-female) were considered quite important. Among the Jews (as early as A.D. 150 to modern times), a prayer was found in which men thanked God that they were not heathen, women, or slaves. S. Scott Bartchy feels this prayer may have been in use during Paul's era. (*First Century Slavery and 1 Corinthians 7:21* [Missoula: Society of Biblical Literature, 1973], pp. 164-165.)

59. The unity "is not one . . . in which ethnic, social and sexual differences vanish, but one in which the barriers, the hostility, the chauvinism, and the sense of superiority and inferiority between respective categories are destroyed." (Charles B. Cousar, *Galatians* [Atlanta: John Knox Press, 1982], p. 86.) Vinay Samuel further points out that the New Testament, as opposed to the Old Testa-

ment, moves in the direction of an inclusive position regarding gender.

60. Bilezikian, *Sex Roles*, p. 128.

61. Some claim Galatians 3:28 merely refers to the equal access to salvation men and women share. However, Klyne R. Snodgrass refutes this claim.

> Christianity did not suddenly grant women access to God that they did not have in Judaism. Women belonged to the covenant in Israel, and Dauzenberg is correct to emphasize that neither the Old Testament nor Judaism saw the categories slave/free or male/female as significant for salvation. . . . The significance of this for our purposes is that one cannot speak of Galatians 3:28 as if it merely pertains to salvation. ("Galatians 3:28: Conundrum or Solution?" *Women, Authority and the Bible*, Alvera Mickelson, ed., [Downers Grove: InterVarsity Press, 1986), p. 178.)

62. Many scholars believe Galatians 3:28 is a normative text. This means that it is a basic teaching, or principle, applicable for all times. It is not a verse limited to a unique, cultural situation. It is a general, unchanging principle. Thus other texts which are not normative (i.e., which are restricted to a historical situation) must be understood in light of the teaching of Galatians 3:28 and not vice versa.

Galatians 6:15-16 seem to confirm this. Verse 15 repeats the theme of the book and the point stressed in 3:28: "Neither circumcision nor uncircumcision means anything; what counts is a new creation." Then in verse 16, Paul refers to this principle as a "rule" (*kanon*). *Kanon* in this passage refers to what is normative for Christians. (H. W. Beyer, "*kanon,* " in *Theological Dictionary of the New Testament*, abridged in one volume by Geoffrey W. Bromiley [Grand Rapids and Devon: Wm. B. Eerdmans Pub. Co. and The Paternoster Press Ltd., 1985], p. 414.)

63. The term "labor" or "work hard" is used to describe these four women. According to Friedrich Hauck, Paul primarily uses this term in reference to "missionary and pastoral work." (*Theological Dictionary of the New Testament*, Gerhard Kittel, ed., Vol. III [Grand Rapids: Wm B. Eerdmans Pub. Co., 1974] pp. 828-829.) While this does not provide conclusive proof, it certainly suggests that these women had a leadership role in the church.

64. James D. G. Dunn, *Word Biblical Commentary*, David A. Hubbard and Glenn W. Barker, eds., Vol. 38 (Dallas: Word Books Pub., 1988), p. 894.

65. Four times out of six, Priscilla's name is mentioned prior to her

husband's. Placing the wife's name first is an unusual order. Bruce M. Metzger indicates that this placement emphasizes Priscilla's prominence. *A Textual Commentary on the Greek New Testament* (London: United Bible Societies, 1971), pp. 466-467.

66. Lesly F. Massey, *Women and the New Testament* (Jefferson: McFarland & Co., Inc., 1989), p. 49.

67. Scanzoni, p. 30.

68. Jack Rogers, p. 325.

69. Evans, p. 65.

70. Bilezikian, *Sex Roles*, p. 137.

71. Gilbert Bilezikian, "A Critical Examination of Wayne Gruden's Treatment of *Kephale* in Ancient Greek Texts," *Women and Men in Ministry: Collected Readings*, Roberta Hestenes, comp. (Pasadena: Fuller Theological Seminary, 1988), p. 141.

72. Henry George Liddell and Robert Scott, *A Greek-English Lexicon*, revised by Henry Stuart Jones, with the assistance of Roderick McKenzie (Oxford: Clarendon Press, 1940), p. 945.

73. Gordon D. Fee, "The First Epistle to the Corinthians," *The New International Commentary on the New Testament*, Vol. 46 (Grand Rapids: Wm. B. Eerdmans Pub. Co., 1987), pp. 502-503; cf. Berkeley and Alvera Mickelsen, "What Does *Kephale* Mean in the New Testament?" *Women, Authority and the Bible*, Alvera Mickelsen, ed. (Downers Grove: InterVarsity Press, 1986), pp. 106-108; Charles Kingsley Barrett, "The First Epistle to the Corinthians," *Harper's New Testament Commentary*, Vol. 7 (New York: Harper & Row Pub., 1968), p. 248; Fritz Reinecker, *Linguistic Key to the Greek New Testament*, Cleon Rogers, trans. (Grand Rapids: Regency Ref. Library, 1976), p. 422.

For further study on the relationship between the Hebrew *ro's* and the Greek *kephale*, see Berkeley and Alvera Mickelsen's article, "What Does *Kephale* Mean in the New Testament?"

74. There are at least two instances in which Christ's headship is related to something other than the church. The first is found in Ephesians 1:22 where Christ is head to everything as well as to the church. The second instance appears in Colossians 2:10. Here Christ is head of every power and authority. In both instances, "source" or "origin" is a suitable definition for head. The idea is that all things, power, and authority have their source and find their completion in him. This thought works well when Ephesians 1:22 is considered alongside Ephesians 1:10, and Colos-

sians 2:10 alongside Colossians 1:16.

75. Bilezikian, *Sex Roles*, p. 161.

76. Evans, p. 76.

77. Bilezikian, *Sex Roles*, p. 161.

78. Mickelsen, p. 107; cf. Bilezikian, *Sex Roles*, pp. 137-139.

79. Bilezikian, *Sex Roles*, p. 138.

80. Ibid.

81. Mickelsen, p. 107; cf. Fee, p. 503.

82. Charles Clayton, Notes, November 1991, WVGB, Great Britain.

83. Rogers, p. 325.

84. Marcus Barth, "Ephesians," *The New International Commentary on the New Testament*, Vol. 2 (New York: Doubleday and Company, Inc., 1974), p. 710.

85. Helen Beard, *Women in Ministry Today* (Plainfield: Logos International, 1980), p. 107.

86. Evans, p. 77.

87. Ibid., p. 154.

88. Beard, p. 111.

89. This interpretation does justice to the meaning of submission (*hupotasso*) when used in the middle form as it is in 1 Peter 3:1. In this form, submission "does not mean so much 'to obey'—though this may result from self-subordination—or to do the will of someone but rather 'to lose or surrender one's own right or will.'" (Halle Gerhard Delling, *Theological Dictionary of the New Testament*, Gerhard Friedrich and Geoffrey Bromiley, eds., Geoffrey Bromiley, trans., Vol. VIII [Grand Rapids: Wm. B. Eerdmans Pub. Co., 1972], p. 40.)

90. Bilezikian, *Sex Roles*, pp. 189-192.

91. *Exousia* is used in connection with Jesus' teaching in Matthew 7:29; 21:23-24, 27; Mark 1:22, 27; 11:28-29, 33; Luke 20:2, 18; 4:32. It is used to refer to his authority to forgive sins in Matthew 9:6, Mark 2:10; Luke 5:24; and of his authority over evil spirits in Luke 4:36; 9:1; and Matthew 9:8.

92. *Kurios* is used in reference to earthly masters in Ephesians 6:5 and in Colossians 3:22 and 4:1. These are the only instances *kurios* is used of church members. However, this does not give masters license to lord it over their slaves. In each of these Scriptures,

qualifications are placed on the master's attitude and actions toward his slave. In addition, Paul provided a precedence in Philemon for the way in which Christian masters and slaves should relate: as dear brothers (Philem. 15-16).

93. C. K. Barrett suggests the possibility that Paul was responding to a Corinthian letter which contained an inquiry on whether or not it was "still necessary to observe conventional distinctions . . . in a community in which there were no longer male and female (Gal. iii.28), and women as well as men were manifestly moved by the Spirit to pray and prophesy (verse 5)" (*Corinthians*, p. 247).

94. Evans, p. 83.

95. Reinecker, p. 422.

96. Gordon D. Fee, *Corinthians*, p. 503.

97. In the Creation account, man is the source of life to woman and not vice versa. This implies their diversity; they are distinct from one another. On the other hand, that woman is *from* man (in creation) implies their unity. She is of the same substance as man.

98. In verses 4 through 6, "head" is used a number of times. There is great variety among scholarship when identifying the metaphorical uses of "head" in these verses. While the author believes that "head" is used literally in every case, it is likely that there is both a literal and figurative use of the term at the end of verse 4. Not only does man dishonor himself when he covers his head to pray and prophesy, but he also brings dishonor to Christ, his head (a reference to v. 3). It's also possible that a dual sense is intended when the term is used a second time in verse 5. However, this does not seem likely since the phrase "dishonors her head" is immediately followed by a clear reference to woman's physical head.

99. Charles H. Talbert offers an interesting contribution in this regard:

> To remove the head covering, moreover, was a symbol of one's transcendence of her sexuality. In *Joseph and Aseneth*, a pre-Christian Hellenistic Jewish propaganda tract, Aseneth is a virgin converted to Judaism through the agency of an archangel. Afterwardshe orders her to remove her clothes of mourning and to put on radiant garments. This she does, including a head covering. When she returns, the angel orders her to take off the head covering, "because you are a holy virgin today and your head is that of a young man." That is, in this Hellenistic Jewish document, Aseneth is believed to have transcended her sexuality as the result of her religious experience. With the transcen-

dence of her femaleness goes the discarding of the social symbol of that sexuality. . . .

Talbert suggests this may have been the case in Corinth. (*Reading Corinthians* [New York: Crossroads, 1987], p. 68.)

100. Ibid., p. 69.

101. Fee, p. 513.

102. In Genesis 1:26-27, woman was clearly created in God's image just as readily as man. While the creation accounts do not say anything about either man or woman being God's glory, the new covenant plainly states that all believers reflect the Lord's glory (2 Cor. 3:18). Woman holds a unique position, for in addition to the above, she is also man's glory.

103. C. M. Ramsay rejects this interpretation, dubbing it "a preposterous idea which a Greek scholar would laugh at anywhere except in the New Testament, where (as they seem to think) Greek words may mean anything that commentators choose." (*The Cities of St. Paul* [New York, 1908], p. 203; cf. Evans, p. 90, and Fee, p. 519.)

104. Evans, pp. 90, 91.

105. Fee, pp. 522, 523.

106. Evans, p. 71.

107. S. Scott Bartchy, "Power, Submission, and Sexual Identity Among Early Christians," *Women and Men in Ministry: Collected Readings*, Roberta Hestenes, comp. (Pasadena: Fuller Theological Seminary, 1988), p. 85.

108. Ibid., p. 95; cf. Reinecker, p. 621.

109. Beard, p. 117.

110. Richard and Catherine Clark Kroeger, "Pandemonium and Silence at Corinth," *Women and Men in Ministry: Collected Readings*, Roberta Hestenes, comp. (Pasadena: Fuller Theological Seminary, 1988), p. 75.

111. Ibid., p. 76.

112. Evans, p. 96.

113. Bentall further strengthens the improbability of this conclusion. She points out that the word "brothers," used throughout the chapter, is a translation of the Greek word *adelphoi*. *Adelphoi* has the same root as the term for sisters, *adelphe*, and one word is easily perceived as addressing both sexes. (p. 35)

114. Many scholars agree that Paul is only limiting a particular form of

participation by the women in the Corinthian church. However, these scholars have differing views about what form of participation is being limited.

Other scholars interpret these verses quite differently. H. Conzelmann sees verses 34 and 35 as a non-Pauline interpolation. (*1 Corinthians*, George W. MacRee, ed., James W. Leitch, trans. [Philadelphia: Fortress Press, 1975], p. 246.) Barrett also suggests this possibility. (*Corinthians*, p. 332.) Others assume that verses 34 and 35 are a quote from a group in the church. Paul quotes them, and in verse 36 disagrees and repudiates them. Bilezikian presents a strong case in this regard. (*Sex Roles*, pp. 144-153.)

115. Jeremias, *Jerusalem*, pp. 373-375.

116. Walter L. Liefeld, "Women, Submission and Ministry in 1 Corinthians," *Women, Authority & the Bible*, Alvera Mickelsen, ed. (Downers Grove: InterVarsity Press, 1986), p. 150.

117. Barrett, *Corinthians*, p. 332.

118. Liefeld, p. 150.

119. The latter has been suggested by Liefeld. (p. 150)

120. Both Evans (p. 98) and Liefeld (p. 151) acknowledge this possibility.

121. McConville, Notes.

122. Evans, p. 95.

123. Liefeld, p. 149.

124. Richard and Catherine Clark Kroeger propose this position, quoting a number of historical evidences. (p. 76)

125. Charles Kingsley Barrett observes, "The sentence [v. 9] contains no verb, and it is best to supply from verse 8 the verb 'to pray,' so that the translation will be, 'In the same way I desire that women should pray, dressed in becoming manner.'" ("Pastoral Epistles," *The New Clarendon Bible* [Oxford: Clarendon Press, 1963], p. 55. So agree Donald Guthrie, "The Pastoral Epistles," *The Tyndale New Testament Commentaries*, R. V. G. Tasker, ed. [Grand Rapids: Wm. B. Eerdmans Pub. Co., 1975], p. 74; Leroy Birney, *Role of Woman in the New Testament Church* [Middlesex: C.B.R.F. Pub., 1971], p. 17; and Evans, p. 101.) The possibility is acknowledged but not necessarily accepted by Archibald Thomas Robertson. ("The Epistles of Paul," *Word Pictures in the New Testament*, Vol. IV [New York: Harper & Brothers Pub., 1931], p. 569.)

Evans makes a further observation: "Verses 8 and 9 are grammatically linked, so that the 'also'—a better translation of *osautos* would be 'likewise'—of verse 9 should be supplemented with 'I wish them to pray.' . . . To see verse 8 as forbidding women to pray would mean that we are presented with a direct parallel between prayer for men and dress for women; a parallel which is not immediately obvious nor seems to be in line with the thought of Paul elsewhere." (p. 101)

126. While the exact nature of the heretical teaching is unknown, it seems that the error had Jewish and possibly Gnostic origins. The pastoral epistles, which deal with these problems, indicate this possibility. 1 Timothy 1:7 speaks of those who want to be "teachers of the law;" in Titus 1:10 some of these are of the circumcision group; Titus 1:14 makes reference to "Jewish myths;" and Titus 3:9 addresses "arguments and quarrels about the law." These suggest the Jewish origin of the false teaching.

Possible Gnostic influences can be found in Titus 3:9 ("foolish controversies and genealogies"); 1 Timothy 4:3, 8 (asceticism); and 1 Timothy 6:20 ("opposing ideas of what is falsely called knowledge"). Ralph Earle observes, "Throughout the Christian world, and especially in intellectual centers such as Ephesus, Alexandria and Rome, there was perhaps not a single educated congregation which did not contain persons infected with some form of Gnosticism." He also points out that early Christian Gnosticism was Jewish in character. (*The Expositor's Bible*, W. Robertson Nicoll, ed., Vol. 54-56 [London: A. C. Armstrong and Son, 1903], pp. 34, 37.) Other Scriptures indicating Paul's concern along this line include 1 Timothy 1:3-4, 19-20; 4:1-5, 7; 6:3-5; 2 Timothy 1:15; 2:15-19, 23; 3:1-9; 4:14-16; and Titus 1:10-16; 2:7-8; 3:9-11.

127. Manuel Miguens, *Church Ministry in New Testament Times* (Arlington: Christian Culture Press, 1976), p. 135.

128. Jeremias brings this point into focus:

[Woman] was exempt from study of the Torah; R. Eliezer (c. A.D. 90), tireless upholder of the old tradition, says impressively, "If a man gives his daughter knowledge of the Law it is as though he taught her lechery" (M. Sot. iii.4). The idea that the Torah should be taught to daughters also (M. Ned. iv.3) and only the oral law kept from them was in no way representative of the old law. In every case, schools were solely for boys, and not girls. Of the two sections of the synagogue mentioned in the law of Augustus . . . , the first, where the liturgical service took place, was open to women too; but the other part, given over to the scribes' teaching, was open only to men and boys as its name suggests. (*Jerusalem*, p. 373.)

129. The word translated "quietness" in verse 11 is a form of the same word translated "quiet" in 2:2. Evans suggests that the injunction to learn in quietness and submission may reflect "the educational ideas of the time regarding the best way of learning" (p. 102).

130. Evans, p. 106. Bilezikian adds that "there are some texts that deliberately open up the teaching ministry to all qualified believers, women included." He cites Colossians 3:16, and points out that the word "teach" used of Paul in Colossians 1:28 is the same word which describes the teaching ministry of all believers in 3:16. Later he concludes with an important insight: "Restrictions to the teaching ministry of the church on the basis of gender are necessarily made with the tacit implication that the authority resides in the teacher rather than in scripture." (*Sex Roles*, pp. 175-177, 184.)

131. Evans, p. 104; Bilezikian, *Sex Roles*, pp. 177, 178.

132. Evans, p. 102; Mark D. Roberts, "Woman Shall Be Saved," *Women and Men in Ministry: Collected Readings*, Roberta Hestenes, comp. (Pasadena: Fuller Theological Seminary, 1988), pp. 66, 68.

133. "The Pastoral Epistles," *Cambridge Greek Testament for Schools and Colleges*, J. Armitage Robinson, ed. (Cambridge: University Press, 1899), p. 48; cf. Guthrie, p. 75; A. T. Robertson suggests "dominate," p. 570; and Barrett, to "domineer over," *Pastoral Epistles*, p. 55.

134. Evans, pp. 103, 104.

135. Ibid., pp. 104, 105.

136. Ibid., p. 104.

137. Bilezikian, *Sex Roles*, p. 183.

138. Roberts, p. 66.

139. Ibid., p. 67.

140. Ibid.

141. Bilezikian, *Sex Roles*, p. 183.

142. Roberta Hestenes, "Women in Leadership: Finding Ways to Serve the Church," *Women and Men in Ministry: Collected Readings*, Roberta Hestenes, comp. (Pasadena: Fuller Theological Seminary, 1988), p. 249.

143. Evans, p. 19.

144. See Romans 16:1; 1 Corinthians 3:5; 2 Corinthians 6:4; 11:23; Eph-

esians 3:7; 6:21; Philippians 1:1; Colossians 1:7, 23, 25; 4:7; 1 Thessalonians 3:2; 1 Timothy 3:8, 12; 4:6.

145. Liddell and Scott, p. 399; Massey, p. 60; Evans, pp. 125, 126; Dunn, pp. 886, 887; Marvin Richardson Vincent, "The Epistles of Paul," *Word Studies in the New Testament*, Vol. III (New York: Charles Scribner's Sons, 1914), pp. 176, 177.

Charles Kingsley Barrett accepts the translation "deaconess" but cautions that the word *diakonos* probably did not have a technical meaning at the time the epistle was written. ("A Commentary on the Epistle to the Romans," *Black's New Testament Commentaries*, Henry Chadwick, ed. [London: Adam & Charles Black, 1957], p. 282.) A similar observation is made by Archibald Robertson, but he still seems to favor "deaconess," and adds that the *Apostolic Constitutions* contains many allusions to deaconesses (p. 425).

146. Robertson, p. 425.

147. Evans, p. 126.

148. B. Reicke, *Theological Dictionary of the New Testament*, Gerhard Friedrich, ed., Geoffrey W. Bromiley, trans., Vol. VI (Grand Rapids: Wm. B. Eerdmans Pub. Co., 1968), p. 703.

149. J. Massyngberde Ford, "Biblical Material Relevant to the Ordination of Women," *Journal of Ecumenical Studies* 10 (Fall 1973): 676, 677.

150. Ibid.

151. Dunn, p. 894.

152. Ibid.

153. Evans, p. 124.

154. Barrett, *Romans*, p. 283; Dunn, p. 894; Robertson agrees the most natural meaning is that they (Andronicus and Junia) were counted among the apostles, but allows for the possibility that they were merely well known to the apostles, p. 427.

155. Dunn, p. 894.

156. Massey, p. 61; Kelly, p. 83.

157. Kelly, p. 83.

158. Ibid.

159. The New Testament lacks a technical word for "deaconess." Thus "deacon" is used for both men and women. In addition to this point, Evans makes the following observation:

It is also important to note that we have in fact very little information about the precise relation between "office" and "function" in the New Testament church. . . . While we learn much about the characteristics required in those who aspire to office, we are told very little about the particular responsibilities and tasks assigned to the holder of any individual office. . . . In fact, in the New Testament, there is no clear distinction made between regulated offices and unregulated ministry by those with no official position. (p. 110)

160. Scanzoni, p. 63.

161. James Strong, *"Dictionary of the Greek New Testament,"* in *The Exhaustive Concordance of the Bible* (New York: The Methodist Book Concern, 1890), p. 51; Reinecker, p. 631.

BIBLIOGRAPHY

Barrett, Charles Kingsley. "A Commentary On the Epistle to the Romans." *Black's New Testament Commentaries*. Edited by Henry Chadwick. London: Adam & Charles Black, 1957.

_____. "The First Epistle to the Corinthians." *Harper's New Testament Commentary*, Vol. 7. New York: Harper & Row Pub., 1968.

_____. "Pastoral Epistles." *The New Clarendon Bible*. Oxford: Clarendon Press, 1963.

Bartchy, S. Scott. "Power, Submission, and Sexual Identity Among Early Christians." *Women and Men in Ministry: Collected Readings*. Compiled by Roberta Hestenes. Pasadena: Fuller Theological Seminary, 1988.

_____. *First Century Slavery and 1 Corinthians 7:21*. Missoula: Society of Biblical Literature, 1973.

Barth, Marcus. "Ephesians." *The New International Commentary on the New Testament*, Vol. 2. New York: Doubleday and Company, Inc., 1974.

Beard, Helen. *Women in Ministry Today*. Plainfield: Logos International, 1980.

Bentall, Shirley F. *What Does God's Word Say to Women Today?* An unpublished paper for the Baptist Women of the Alberta Area, 1983.

Beyer, H. W, "Kanon," in *Theological Dictionary of the New Testament*, abridged in one volume by Geoffrey W. Bromiley. Grand Rapids and Devon: Wm. B. Eerdmans Pub. Co. and The Paternoster Press, 1985.

Bilezikian, Gilbert. *Beyond Sex Roles*. Grand Rapids: Baker Book House, 1986.

_____. "A Critical Examination of Wayne Gruden's Treatment of 'Kephale' In Ancient Greek Texts." *Women and Men in Ministry: Collected Readings*. Compiled by Roberta Hestenes. Pasadena: Fuller

Theological Seminary, 1988.

Birney, Leroy. *Role of Woman In the New Testament Church*. Middlesex: C. B. R. F. Pub., 1971.

Brown, Francis, S. R. Driver, and C.A. Briggs, eds. *Hebrew and English Lexicon of the Old Testament*. Oxford: Clarendon Press, 1907.

Brown, Stephen James M. *Image and Truth: Studies in the Imagery of the Bible*. Rome: Catholic Book Agency, 1955.

Caird, George Bradford. *The Language and Imagery of the Bible*. Philadelphia: The Westminster Press, 1980.

Collins, Sheila D. *A Different Heaven and Earth*. Valley Forge: Judson Press, 1974.

Conzelmann, H. *I Corinthians*. Edited by George W. MacRee. Translated by James W. Leitch. Philadelphia: Fortress Press, 1975.

Cousar, Charles B. *Galatians*. Atlanta: John Knox Press, 1982.

Delling, Halle Gerhard. *Theological Dictionary of the New Testament*, Vol. VIII. Edited by Gerhard Friedrich and Geoffrey Bromiley. Translated by Geoffrey Bromiley. Grand Rapids: Wm. B. Eerdmans Pub. Co., 1972.

Dunn, James D. G. *Word Biblical Commentary*. Edited by David A. Hubbard and Glenn W. Barker. Vol. 38. Dallas: Word Books, Pub., 1988.

Earle, Ralph. *The Expositor's Bible*, Vol. 54-56. Edited by W. Robertson Nicoll. London: A. C. Armstrong and Son, 1903.

Evans, Mary J. *Women in the Bible*. Downers Grove: InterVarsity Press, 1983.

Fee, Gordon D. "The First Epistle to the Corinthians." *The New International Commentary On the New Testament*, Vol. 46. Grand Rapids: Wm. B. Eerdmans Pub. Co., 1987.

Ford, J. Massyngberde. "Biblical Material Relevant to the Ordination of Women." *Journal of Ecumenical Studies* 10 (Fall 1973).

Guthrie, Donald. "The Pastoral Epistles." *The Tyndale New Testament Commentaries*. Edited by R.V.G. Tasker. Grand Rapids: Wm. B. Eerdmans Pub. Co., 1975.

Hauck, Friedrich. *Theological Dictionary of the New Testament*, Vol. III. Edited by Gerhard Kittel. Grand Rapids: Wm. B. Eerdmans, 1974.

Hendriksen, William. "Exposition of Galatians." *New Testament Commentary*, Vol. 9. Grand Rapids: Baker Book House, 1968.

Hestenes, Roberta. "Women in Leadership: Finding Ways to Serve the

Church." *Women and Men in Ministry: Collected Readings*. Compiled by Roberta Hestenes. Pasadena: Fuller Theological Seminary, 1988.

Howe, E. Margaret. *Women and Church Leadership*. Grand Rapids: Zondervan Pub. House, 1982.

Jeremias, Joachim. *Jerusalem in the Time of Jesus*. Philadelphia: Fortress Press, 1969.

_____. "Anthropos," in *The Theological Dictionary of the New Testament*. Abridged in one volume by Geoffrey W. Bromiley. Grand Rapids and Devon: Wm. B. Eerdmans Pub. Co. and The Paternoster Press Ltd., 1985.

Jewett, Paul King. *Man As Male and Female*. Grand Rapids: Wm. B. Eerdmans Pub. Co., 1975.

_____. *The Ordination of Women*. Grand Rapids: Wm. B. Eerdmans Pub. Co., 1980.

Keil, C.F. & F. Delitzsch. "The Pentateuch." *Biblical Commentary on the Old Testament*, Vol. 1. Translated by James Martin. Edinburgh: T. & T. Clark, 1864.

Kelly, John Norman Davidson. "A Commentary On the Pastoral Epistles." *Harper's New Testament Commentaries*, Vol. 13. New York and Evanston: Harper & Row, Pub., 1963.

Köhler, Ludwig Hugo. *Old Testament Theology*. Translated by A. S. Todd. Philadelphia: The Westminster Press, 1957.

Kroeger, Richard and Catherine Clark. "Pandemonium and Silence at Corinth." *Women and Men In Ministry: Collected Readings*. Compiled by Roberta Hestenes. Pasadena: Fuller Theological Seminary, 1988.

Liddell, Henry George and Robert Scott. *A Greek-English Lexicon*. Revised by Henry Stuart Jones, with the assistance of Roderick McKenzie. Oxford: Clarendon Press, 1940.

Liefeld, Walter L. "Women, Submission and Ministry in I Corinthians." *Women, Authority and The Bible*. Edited by Alvera Mickelsen. Downers Grove: InterVarsity Press, 1986.

MacHaffie, Barbara J. *Her Story*. Philadelphia: Fortress Press, 1986.

Massey, Lesly F. *Women and the New Testament*. Jefferson: McFarland & Co., Inc., 1989.

Metzger, Bruce M. *A Textual Commentary on the Greek New Testament*. London: United Bible Societies, 1971.

Mickelsen, Berkeley and Alvera. "What Does 'Kephale' Mean in the New Testament?" *Women, Authority and the Bible*. Edited by Alvera Mickelsen. Downers Grove: Intervarsity Press, 1986.

Miguens, Manuel. *Church Ministry in New Testament Times*. Arlington: Christian Culture Press, 1976.

Murray, John. "The Epistle to the Romans." *The New International Commentary on the New Testament*, Vol. 2. Edited by F. F. Bruce. Introduction by John Murray. Grand Rapids: Wm. B. Eerdmans Pub. Co., 1965.

Oepke, A. "Aner" in *The Theological Dictionary of the New Testament*. Abridged in one volume by Geoffrey W. Bromiley. Grand Rapids and Devon: Wm. B. Eerdmans Pub. Co. and The Paternoster Press Ltd., 1985.

Ramsay, C.M. *The Cities of St. Paul*. New York, 1908.

Reicke, B. *Theological Dictionary of the New Testament*, Vol. VI. Edited by Gerhard Friedrich. Translated by Geoffrey W. Bromiley. Grand Rapids: Wm. B. Eerdmans Pub. Co., 1968.

Reinecker, Fritz. *Linguistic Key to the Greek New Testament*. Translated by Cleon Rogers. Grand Rapids: Regency Ref. Library, 1976.

Roberts, Mark. D. "Woman Shall Be Saved." *Women and Men in Ministry: Collected Readings*. Compiled by Roberta Hestenes. Pasadena: Fuller Theological Seminary, 1988.

Robertson, Archibald Thomas. "The Epistles of Paul." *Word Pictures in the New Testament*, Vol. IV. New York: Harper & Brothers Pub., 1931.

Robinson, J. Armitage, ed. "The Pastoral Epistles." *Cambridge Greek Testament for Schools and Colleges*. Cambridge: University Press, 1899.

Rogers, Jack. "The Kenyon Case." *Women and Men in Ministry: Collected Readings*. Compiled by Roberta Hestenes. Pasadena: Fuller Theological Seminary, 1988.

Sarna, Nahum M. "Genesis." *The J. P. S. Torah Commentary*, Vol. 2. Philadelphia: The Jewish Publication Society, 1989.

Sayers, Dorothy. *Are Women Human?* Grand Rapids: Wm. B. Eerdmans Pub. Co., 1971.

Scanzoni, Letha, and Nancy Hardesty. *All We're Meant to Be*. Waco: Word Books Pub., 1974.

Scholer, David M. "1 Timothy 2:9-15 & the Place of Women in the Church's Ministry." *Women, Authority and the Bible*. Edited by Alvera Mickelsen. Downers Grove: InterVarsity Press, 1986.

Smalley, Gary, and John Trent. *The Blessing*. Nashville: Thomas Nelson Publishers, 1986.

Snodgrass, Klyne R. "Galatians 3:28: Conundrum or Solution?" *Women, Authority and the Bible.* Edited by Alvera Mickelsen. Downers Grove: InterVarsity Press, 1986.

Spencer, Aida Besancon. *Beyond the Curse.* Nashville: Thomas Nelson Publishers, 1985.

Strong, James. "Dictionary of the Greek New Testament" in *The Exhaustive Concordance of the Bible.* New York: The Methodist Book Concern, 1890.

Swidler, Leonard J. *Biblical Affirmations of Women.* Philadelphia: The Westminster Press, 1979.

Talbert, Charles H. *Reading Corinthians.* New York: Crossroads, 1987.

Vincent, Marvin Richardson. *Word Studies In the New Testament,* Vol. IV. New York: Charles Scribner's Sons, 1914.

_____. "The Epistles of Paul." *Word Studies In the New Testament,* Vol. III. New York: Charles Scribner's Sons, 1914.

Webster's Third New International Dictionary. Springfield: Merriam-Webster, Inc., 1981.

Westermann, Claus. *Genesis 1-11: A Commentary.* Translated by John J. Scullion, S.J. Minneapolis: Augsburg Pub. House, 1984.

Wigram, George V. *The New Englishman's Concordance.* Peabody: Hendrickson Pub., Inc., 1984.

Williams, Don. *The Apostle Paul and Women in the Church.* Van Nuys: Bim Pub. Co., 1977.

Wilson, William. *New Wilson's Old Testament Word Studies.* Grand Rapids: Kregel Publications, 1987.

MARC Publications

Bringing you key resources on the world mission of the church

MARC books and other publications support the work of MARC
(Mission Advanced Research and Communications Center), which
is to inspire fresh vision and to empower the Christian mission
among those who extend the whole gospel to the whole world.

Recent MARC titles include

❏ *Mission Handbook*. The 1993-95 Edition continues as the most
comprehensive available listing of Christan mission agencies
based in North America, with detailed up-to-date descriptions
and statistics, analysis and essays. "The Changing Shape of
World Mission" presents in color graphics the challenge before
missions globally. Also available in a powerful IBM-compatible
computer software version. Ask for details.

❏ *The Catholic Church in Mission*, Eugene Daniels. A Protes-
tant looks seriously at the Roman Catholic Church's official
teaching concerning the Christian mission. A concise summary
of the church's modern documents.

❏ *Facing the Powers*, Thomas H. McAlpine. Surveys 16 contemporary mission thinkers regarding the nature and operation of
the "principalities and powers," and the implications for the
mission community.

❏ *The Spirit Said 'Grow'*, Vinson Synan. Details the worldwide
growth of the charismatic and Pentecostal churches.

❏ *Empowering the Poor*, Robert C. Linthicum. A bold Christian
strategy for community organizing in the urban context.

MARC

A division of World Vision International
121 E. Huntington Drive, Monrovia CA 91016-3400
Phone (818)303-8811
or call toll-free in USA: 1-800-777-7752
VISA AND MASTERCARD ACCEPTED

Ask for the MARC Newsletter and complete publications list.